204
B

Boy
Yos

ELEANOR ROOSEVELT

ELEANOR ROOSEVELT

RACHEL TOOR

CHELSEA HOUSE PUBLISHERS

NEW YORK • PHILADELPHIA

CHELSEA HOUSE PUBLISHERS
EDITOR-IN-CHIEF: Nancy Toff
EXECUTIVE EDITOR: Remmel T. Nunn
MANAGING EDITOR: Karyn Gullen Browne
COPY CHIEF: Juliann Barbato
PICTURE EDITOR: Adrian G. Allen
ART DIRECTOR: Maria Epes
MANUFACTURING MANAGER: Gerald Levine

American Women of Achievement
SENIOR EDITOR: Constance Jones

Staff for ELEANOR ROOSEVELT
ASSOCIATE EDITOR: Maria Behan
DEPUTY COPY CHIEF: Ellen Scordato
EDITORIAL ASSISTANT: Heather Lewis
PICTURE RESEARCHER: Andrea Reithmayr
ASSISTANT ART DIRECTOR: Laurie Jewell
DESIGN: Design Oasis
DESIGNER: Donna Sinisgalli
PRODUCTION COORDINATOR: Joseph Romano
COVER ILLUSTRATOR: Vilma Ortiz

3   5   7   9   8   6   4   2

Library of Congress Cataloging-in-Publication Data

Toor, Rachel.
  Eleanor Roosevelt / Rachel Toor.
    p.   cm.—(American women of achievement)
  Bibliography: p.
  Includes index.
  ISBN 1-55546-674-5.
      0-7910-0449-X (pbk.)
  1. Roosevelt, Eleanor, 1884–1962—Juvenile literature.
2. Presidents—United States—Wives—Biography—Juvenile litera-
ture.
I. Title. II. Series.
E807.1.R48T66 1989
973.917′092′4—dc19   88-25725
  [B]   CIP

CONTENTS

AMERICAN WOMEN of ACHIEVEMENT

Abigail Adams
women's rights advocate

Jane Addams
social worker

Louisa May Alcott
author

Marian Anderson
singer

Susan B. Anthony
woman suffragist

Ethel Barrymore
actress

Clara Barton
founder of the American Red Cross

Elizabeth Blackwell
physician

Nellie Bly
journalist

Margaret Bourke-White
photographer

Pearl Buck
author

Rachel Carson
biologist and author

Mary Cassatt
artist

Agnes De Mille
choreographer

Emily Dickinson
poet

Isadora Duncan
dancer

Amelia Earhart
aviator

Mary Baker Eddy
founder of the Christian Science church

Betty Friedan
feminist

Althea Gibson
tennis champion

Emma Goldman
political activist

Helen Hayes
actress

Lillian Hellman
playwright

Katharine Hepburn
actress

Karen Horney
psychoanalyst

Anne Hutchinson
religious leader

Mahalia Jackson
gospel singer

Helen Keller
humanitarian

Jeane Kirkpatrick
diplomat

Emma Lazarus
poet

Clare Boothe Luce
author and diplomat

Barbara McClintock
biologist

Margaret Mead
anthropologist

Edna St. Vincent Millay
poet

Julia Morgan
architect

Grandma Moses
painter

Louise Nevelson
sculptor

Sandra Day O'Connor
Supreme Court justice

Georgia O'Keeffe
painter

Eleanor Roosevelt
diplomat and humanitarian

Wilma Rudolph
champion athlete

Florence Sabin
medical researcher

Beverly Sills
opera singer

Gertrude Stein
author

Gloria Steinem
feminist

Harriet Beecher Stowe
author and abolitionist

Mae West
entertainer

Edith Wharton
author

Phillis Wheatley
poet

Babe Didrikson Zaharias
champion athlete

CHELSEA HOUSE PUBLISHERS

"Remember the Ladies"

MATINA S. HORNER

Remember the Ladies." That is what Abigail Adams wrote to her husband John, then a delegate to the Continental Congress, as the Founding Fathers met in Philadelphia to form a new nation in March of 1776. "Be more generous and favorable to them than your ancestors. Do not put such unlimited power in the hands of the Husbands. If particular care and attention is not paid to the Ladies," Abigail Adams warned, "we are determined to foment a Rebellion, and will not hold ourselves bound by any Laws in which we have no voice, or Representation."

The words of Abigail Adams, one of the earliest American advocates of women's rights, were prophetic. Because when we have not "remembered the ladies," they have, by their words and deeds, reminded us so forcefully of the omission that we cannot fail to remember them. For the history of American women is as interesting and varied as the history of our nation as a whole. American women have played an integral part in founding, settling, and building our country. Some we remember as remarkable women who—against great odds—achieved distinction in the public arena: Anne Hutchinson, who in the 17th century became a charismatic religious leader; Phillis Wheatley, an 18th-century black slave who became a poet; Susan B. Anthony, whose name is synonymous with the 19th-century women's rights movement, and who led the struggle to enfranchise women; and, in our own century, Amelia Earhart, the first woman to cross the Atlantic Ocean by air.

These extraordinary women certainly merit our admiration, but other women, "common women," many of them all but forgotten, should also be recognized for their contributions to American thought and culture. Women have been community builders; they have founded schools and formed voluntary associations to help those in need; they have assumed the major responsibility for rearing children, passing on from one generation to the next the values that keep a culture alive. These and innumerable other contributions, once ignored, are now being recognized by scholars, students, and the public. It is exciting and gratifying to realize that a part of our history that was hardly acknowledged a few generations ago is now being studied and brought to light.

In recent decades, the field of women's history has grown from obscurity to a politically controversial splinter movement to academic respectability, in many cases mainstreamed into such traditional disciplines as history, economics, and psychology. Scholars of women, both female and male, have organized research centers at such prestigious institutions as Wellesley College, Stanford University, and the University of California. Other notable centers for women's studies are the Center for the American Woman and Politics at the Eagleton Institute of Politics at Rutgers University; the Henry A. Murray Research Center for the Study of Lives, at Radcliffe College; and the Women's Research and Education Institute, the research arm of the Congressional Caucus on Women's Issues. Other scholars and public figures have established archives and libraries, such as the Schlesinger Library on the History of Women in America, at Radcliffe College, and the Sophia Smith Collection, at Smith College, to collect and preserve the written and tangible legacies of women.

From the initial donation of the Women's Rights Collection in 1943, the Schlesinger Library grew to encompass vast collections documenting the manifold accomplishments of American women. Simultaneously, the women's movement in general and the academic discipline of women's studies in particular also began with a narrow definition and gradually expanded their mandate. Early causes such as woman suffrage and social reform, abolition and organized labor were joined by newer concerns such as the history of women in business and the professions and in politics and government; the study of the family; and social issues such as health policy and education.

Women, as historian Arthur M. Schlesinger, jr., once pointed out, "have constituted the most spectacular casualty of traditional history. They have made up at least half the human race, but you could never tell that by looking at the books historians write." The new breed of historians is remedying that omission. They have written books about immigrant women and about working-class women who struggled for survival in cities and about black women who met the challenges of life in rural areas. They are telling the stories of women who, despite the barriers of tradition and economics, became lawyers and doctors and public figures.

The women's studies movement has also led scholars to question traditional interpretations of their respective disciplines. For example, the study of war has traditionally been an exercise in military and political analysis, an examination of strategies planned and executed by men. But scholars of women's history have pointed out that wars have also been periods of tremendous change and even opportunity for women, because the very absence of men on the home front enabled them to expand their educational, economic, and professional activities and to assume leadership in their homes.

The early scholars of women's history showed a unique brand of courage in choosing to investigate new subjects and take new approaches to old ones. Often, like their subjects, they endured criticism and even ostracism by their academic colleagues. But their efforts have unquestionably been worthwhile, because with the publication of each new study and book another piece of the historical patchwork is sewn into place, revealing an increasingly comprehensive picture of the role of women in our rich and varied history.

Such books on groups of women are essential, but books that focus on the lives of individuals are equally indispensable. Biographies can be inspirational, offering their readers the example of people with vision who have looked outside themselves for their goals and have often struggled against great obstacles to achieve them. Marian Anderson, for instance, had to overcome racial bigotry in order to perfect her art and perform as a concert singer. Isadora Duncan defied the rules of classical dance to find true artistic freedom. Jane Addams had to break down society's notions of the proper role for women in order to create new social institutions, notably the settlement house. All of these women had to come to terms both with themselves and with the world in which they lived. Only then could they move ahead as pioneers in their chosen callings.

Biography can inspire not only by adulation but also by realism. It helps us to see not only the qualities in others that we hope to emulate, but also, perhaps, the weaknesses that made them "human." By helping us identify with the subject on a more personal level they help us to feel that we, too, can achieve such goals. We read about Eleanor Roosevelt, for instance, who occupied a unique and seemingly enviable position as the wife of the president. Yet we can sympathize with her inner dilemma: an inherently shy woman, she had to force herself to live a most public life in order to use her position to benefit others. We may not be able to imagine ourselves having the immense poetic talent of Emily Dickinson, but from her story we can understand the challenges faced by a creative woman who was expected to fulfill many family responsibilities. And though few of us will ever reach the level of athletic accomplishment displayed by Wilma Rudolph or Babe Zaharias, we can still appreciate their spirit, their overwhelming will to excel.

A biography is a multifaceted lens. It is first of all a magnification, the intimate examination of one particular life. But at the same time, it is a wide-angle lens, informing us about the world in which the subject lived. We come away from reading about one life knowing more about the social, political, and economic fabric of the time. It is for this reason, perhaps, that the great New England essayist Ralph Waldo Emerson wrote, in 1841, "There is properly no history: only biography." And it is also why biography, and particularly women's biography, will continue to fascinate writers and readers alike.

ELEANOR ROOSEVELT

In 1933 Eleanor Roosevelt became first lady of the United States. Six years later she protested the racist treatment of black singer Marian Anderson by the Daughters of the American Revolution.

ONE

A Concert in Washington

It was early 1939 and First Lady Eleanor Roosevelt found herself in a difficult position. She had just learned that a group she belonged to—the Daughters of the American Revolution—practiced racial discrimination. The DAR, as the organization was popularly known, was made up of women from old, prominent American families. Roosevelt had long supported the group's patriotism; now she was shocked and disappointed to learn that some members of the DAR were bigots as well as patriots.

The organization had recently denied world-renowned singer Marian Anderson the right to present a concert at Constitution Hall, the only auditorium in Washington, D.C., large enough to hold the large crowd expected to turn out for her performance. The singer's tremendous popularity and stature as an artist would have guaranteed her a place on Constitution Hall's roster of events but for one fact: Marian Anderson was black. The DAR refused to allow any black performer to appear on its stage.

As a public figure, Eleanor Roosevelt was outraged by the group's decision. But the incident also upset her on a personal level, because she knew and admired Anderson, whom she had invited to sing at the White House a few years earlier. Although presidents' wives were generally expected to stay in the background, Roosevelt did not fit this mold. She was a woman of principle, and she knew she must act on her ideals once again. The only question in her mind was how she could best combat the unabashedly racist position taken by the DAR.

Roosevelt had a unique platform

A man drinks from a Colored Only water fountain. Roosevelt opposed the racial segregation common throughout the United States in the first half of the 20th century.

from which to discuss her dilemma. Unlike any first lady before—or since—she wrote a daily syndicated newspaper column. "My Day" by Eleanor Roosevelt was read avidly nationwide. On February 27, 1939, she used this forum to take on the DAR:

I have been debating in my mind for some time a question which I have had to debate with myself once or twice before in my life. Usually I have decided differently from the way I am deciding now. The question is, if you belong to an organization and disapprove of an

action which is typical of a policy, should you resign or is it better to work for a changed point of view within the organization? In the past, when I was able to work actively in any organization to which I belonged, I have usually stayed in until I had at least made a fight and been defeated.

Even then, I have, as a rule, accepted my defeat and decided I was wrong, or, perhaps, a little too far ahead of the thinking of the majority at that time. I have often found that the thing in which I was interested was done some years later. But, in this case, I belong to an organization in which I can do no active work. They have taken an action which has been widely talked of in the press. To remain as a member implies approval of that action, and therefore I am resigning.

Eleanor Roosevelt was first and foremost a practical woman, and as she had in the past, she had tailored her response to the situation. Several years earlier, when a New York women's club refused to admit one of Roosevelt's good friends, the members all knew that the exclusion had been made because the woman was Jewish. The reason behind the decision was never stated, but it was understood. Roosevelt quietly resigned from the club, in the belief that creating a stir would only inflame the anti-Semitism of the other members and create resentment. But the DAR issue, she decided, was different. Because the policy was public knowledge, she felt she should seize the opportunity to encourage all Americans to examine their attitudes about race.

Anderson's plight—and Roosevelt's response to it—immediately became international news. Walter White, head of the National Association for the Advancement of Colored People (NAACP), noted that Roosevelt's public resignation from the DAR "focused worldwide attention on the episode." Some individuals criticized her decision, but most people applauded it. A Gallup poll showed that 67 percent of those questioned at the time supported the first lady's stand. A committed Democrat, Roosevelt received the support of ranking party leaders and was deluged with letters of praise from friends, relatives, and strangers. Even her Republican cousin Corinne Alsop—who disagreed with her on all political mat-

Roosevelt and educator Mary McLeod Bethune address a black youth conference in 1939. Unlike any first lady before her, Roosevelt vigorously pressed for social change.

ters—commended her. "I want you to know how proud I was of you the other day," Alsop wrote Roosevelt. "You are the first lady of the land in your own right."

Roosevelt's actions encouraged Walter White and Anderson's manager, Sol Hurok, to pursue the idea of staging a concert in Washington. Roosevelt also seems to have been partly behind the plan that Hurok and White finally worked out with the government. On Easter Sunday Anderson would give a free, open-air concert at a particularly appropriate spot—the Lincoln Memorial.

On April 9, 1939, an estimated 75,000 people gathered in Washington, D.C., to hear Marian Anderson sing. Standing before the towering image of Abraham Lincoln, the president who had freed America's slaves, the contralto opened her concert with a soaring version of "America." She closed her recital with "Nobody Knows the Trouble I've Seen," a moving spiritual that had a special meaning in light of Anderson's struggle to be heard in the nation's capital.

When the concert was over, Walter White sent a letter to Eleanor Roosevelt. "Thanks in large measure to you,"

A crowd of 75,000 gathers for Marian Anderson's Washington concert. Because the DAR denied the singer the use of its stage, the event was held at the Lincoln Memorial.

17

he wrote, "the Marian Anderson concert on Sunday was one of the most thrilling experiences of our time. Only one thing marred it—that you couldn't be there." Roosevelt was aware that she had already crossed the boundaries that usually restricted presidents' wives. She decided to keep a low profile and did not attend the concert. But by taking a public stand, she had done her part to redress racial injustice—and to make sure that Marian Anderson had her day.

Eleanor Roosevelt's role in the Anderson incident was typical of a lifetime devoted to humanitarian principles. First as a young volunteer worker, then as first lady, and finally as a delegate to the United Nations, she consistently showed a willingness to

Secretary of the Interior Harold Ickes congratulates Anderson on April 9, 1939, the day of her historic Washington concert.

Roosevelt speaks on the changing roles of women. Because of her involvement in causes ranging from civil rights to feminism, she was America's most controversial first lady.

act on her beliefs. A tireless activist, she was bent on doing all she could to further the progress of the society in which she lived. Her outspoken advocacy of such controversial causes as women's rights and the creation of the nation of Israel brought her many detractors, but it also made her one of the world's most admired women. Despite her gracious, self-effacing manner, she was probably the most powerful American woman of her era.

Elliott Roosevelt gazes fondly at his four-year-old daughter Eleanor in 1889. Loving yet unpredictable, Roosevelt contributed to his shy child's insecurities.

TWO

A Girl Called "Granny"

At the end of the 19th century New York City's "high society" was made up of a small circle of wealthy, prominent families. Their children grew up together, attended parties together, and eventually married each other to start the cycle over again. Young women were expected to be pretty, well dressed, and demure; young men tried to appear handsome, prosperous, and witty.

Eleanor Roosevelt's parents embodied these ideals of upperclass elegance. When Elliott Roosevelt, a good-looking young businessman, met 18-year-old Anna Rebecca Hall, she was the most popular debutante in New York. He was captivated right away by Hall, a young woman he described as "a tall slender fair-haired little beauty." The press dubbed their December 1, 1882, marriage "one of the most brilliant social events of the season." The Roosevelts and their friends set the latest fashions, frequented the gala balls typical of the period, and appeared regularly in the society columns.

Anna Eleanor Roosevelt always felt out of place in the glittering world into which she was born on October 11, 1884. Quiet, reserved Eleanor had very little confidence in herself, and Anna Roosevelt's habit of poking fun at her daughter's serious nature by calling her "Granny" hardly boosted the young girl's flagging self-esteem. "She often called me that," Eleanor Roosevelt wrote years later, "for I was a solemn child, without beauty and painfully shy and I seemed like a little old woman entirely lacking in the spontaneous joy and mirth of youth."

Despite the differences in their char-

Anna Hall Roosevelt, Eleanor's beautiful mother, teasingly called her daughter "Granny" because of Eleanor's serious nature.

acters, Eleanor grew close to her irresponsible, high-spirited father. She later remarked that he was "the one great love of my life as a child . . . and I never doubted that I stood first in his heart." Her relationship with Elliott Roosevelt was complicated, however. A wild and adventuresome young man, he was often moody, depressed, and in poor health—conditions that worsened with the heavy drinking in which he often indulged. His mood swings and occasional disappearances puzzled and frightened Eleanor. From overheard conversations, she gleaned that "something was wrong with my father."

The Roosevelt clan expanded five years after Eleanor's birth when her brother Elliott, Jr., arrived. Like most wealthy children of the era, the youngsters were tended by governesses and saw little of their mother, even less of their father. The responsibilities of his growing family failed to sober Elliott Roosevelt. He was drinking heavily and had repeatedly threatened to kill himself. In 1890 the family began an extended visit to Europe in the hope that a change of scene would enable him to break free from his alcoholism.

The Roosevelts visited Germany, Austria, Italy, and France. Initially, the trip seemed to restore Eleanor's father, and the future looked bright when Anna Roosevelt became pregnant with her third and last child, a son they named Hall. But soon after Hall's birth in 1891, Elliott Roosevelt resumed his old bad habits: He began an affair with another woman, disappeared for days at a time, and, most ominously, drank to excess. Frightened by his black moods and erratic behavior, a desperate Anna Roosevelt finally had him confined to an asylum to force him to accept medical treatment.

After his release from the French hospital, Elliott Roosevelt returned to the United States—but not to his family. His wife had insisted on a one-year separation. After years of broken promises and disappointments, she wanted concrete proof that her husband had broken the cycle of alcoholism before he rejoined his family. Elliott Roosevelt went to Illinois to undertake yet another cure for his drinking problem, then to Virginia, where he managed one of his brother-in-law's coal mines. Eleanor desperately missed her beloved father and resented her mother, whom she blamed for driving him away. At her family's homes in New York City and Bar Harbor, Maine, the young girl grew more and more withdrawn.

Eleanor began her formal education in 1892, when Anna Roosevelt hired a private tutor to come to the house to instruct her daughter and a few other neighborhood girls. Although she had impressed adults with her intelligence and creativity, she was initially a poor student who stumbled over even simple questions. Eleanor Roosevelt's memoirs revealed the reason behind her poor performance: Anna Roosevelt sat in on the lessons, and her presence made her daughter nervous.

During this period Anna Roosevelt's health began to deteriorate. She suffered from headaches and excruciating backaches that left her bedridden for days at a time. Eight-year-old Eleanor was determined to take care of her ailing mother and spent hours tending her and massaging her aching temples. Years later she remarked, "Feeling that I was useful was perhaps the greatest joy I experienced."

But when Anna Roosevelt came down with diphtheria, she was beyond her daughter's help. The exiled Elliott Roosevelt begged to be allowed to return to see his failing wife, but Mary Ludlow Hall, his disapproving mother-in-law, refused his request. It was only after Anna Roosevelt died on December 7, 1892, that her devastated husband returned to New York. "Death

Roosevelt biographer Joseph Lash commented that Eleanor's unhappy childhood "gave her a profound sense of kinship with all lonely, deprived, and excluded youngsters."

Elliott Roosevelt sits with Eleanor and Elliott, Jr., during the family's 1890 visit to Germany. This trip was an unsuccessful attempt to cure Elliott's alcoholism.

meant nothing to me," Eleanor recalled years later, "and one fact wiped out everything else—my father was back and I would see him very soon."

When Eleanor finally saw her father again, the meeting was an emotional one. Elliott Roosevelt promised his daughter that they would soon be a family again and spoke of the wonderful things they would do and the exotic places they would see. Looking back on this meeting, Eleanor Roosevelt recalled, "There started that day a feeling which never left me, that he and I were

very close and someday would have a life of our own together."

But the long-anticipated reunion proved to be short-lived. Fearing her husband's irresponsibility, Anna Roosevelt had left a will that granted her mother custody of her three children. At Grandmother Hall's house on West 37th Street, Eleanor felt more alienated and alone than ever before. With no parents around, she tried to protect and care for her younger brothers. But her feelings of helplessness were reinforced in May 1893 when scarlet fever struck the household. Both her brothers contracted the illness, and Elliott, Jr., succumbed to it.

Eleanor saw her father only occasionally, and the little time they spent together was often fraught with anxiety. On some days Elliott Roosevelt would be the loving parent she longed for; on others he would be irrational and undependable. "One day," she remembered, "he took me and three of his fox terriers and left us with the doorman at the Knickerbocker Club. When he failed to return after six hours, the doorman took me home."

On August 14, 1894, Elliott Roosevelt suffered a fatal fall during a drinking bout. He died a broken and lonely man. A New York newspaper reported that, "Even the landlord from whom he rented his house knew him only as Mr. Elliott. Under that name he had lived there with his valet for over ten months. He sought absolute seclu-

This photograph was taken in 1892, the year that Eleanor and her brothers, Elliott, Jr. (left), and Hall, lost their mother to diphtheria.

sion." The account closed with a poignant reminder of how much things had changed for Eleanor's family over the past several years: "There was a time when there were not many more popular young persons in society than Mr. and Mrs. Elliott Roosevelt."

Eleanor carried conflicting memories of her father with her for the rest of her life. "He dominated my life as long as he lived," she later said of her father, "and was the love of my life for many years after he died." The legacy of his love—and his irresponsibility—shaped both her youth and adulthood. As she grew older, she sought to become the type of kind, strong woman he had wanted her to be. Yet at the same time, the memory of his weakness and unreliability left her wary and insecure. It seems likely that her painful youth engendered the compassion that would be her trademark in later years.

25

With the death of her father, Eleanor began to lose hope that she would ever escape from Grandmother Hall's stern household. She, her brother, and her grandmother shared their home with her mother's four brothers and sisters, all of them young adults. Her aunts and uncles often showed little interest in their niece, and Eleanor faded into the background. Years later her cousin Corinne Robinson described visits to the Hall mansion: "I never wanted to go. The grim atmosphere of that house. There was no place to play games, unbroken gloom everywhere. We ate our suppers in silence. The general attitude was 'don't do this.' "

Grandmother Hall had little trouble restraining Eleanor, a somber little girl more interested in pursuing her studies than in frivolity. She continued with the lessons set up by her mother, and she began to excel as a student. But society valued charm more than intelligence in young girls, and Eleanor felt that her looks and social skills were inferior to her friends'. Grandmother Hall dressed her in shapeless, unattractive dresses that did nothing to flatter her gangling figure. Comparing herself to her memory of her lively, beautiful mother, she always felt inadequate. Based on photographs of Eleanor as a girl, it seems that she was quite attractive, but she saw herself as homely. Unless she was doing something to help, something useful, she felt she had nothing to offer. Her

cousin Corinne remembered, "We were a gay ebullient family. Eleanor was just sad."

But Eleanor Roosevelt had several means of escape from her often dreary childhood. She was a voracious reader and often went for long rambles near the Halls' summer house on New York's Hudson River. She and her brother sometimes staged impromptu plays; other days, she was able to convince one of her aunts to take her for a boat ride. A rare treat was a visit with her father's brother, Theodore Roosevelt, who would become president of the United States in 1901. Eleanor was his favorite niece, and he often spent a great deal of time playing with the children during her visits. At Uncle Teddy's house she was encouraged to engage in the rough-and-tumble child's play forbidden at Grandmother Hall's. According to her memoirs, she found these visits both frightening and exhilarating.

Eleanor's life changed when she was 15 years old and Grandmother Hall sent her to Allenswood, a girls' boarding school outside of London, England. This establishment, which catered to a wealthy international clientele, was run by a Frenchwoman named Marie Souvestre. Souvestre served as an important role model for her students, who fondly referred to her as "Sou."

Souvestre was a remarkable woman who had a profound influence on Eleanor. She stressed independent think-

Eleanor walks a pony at her grandmother Hall's country estate. Hall became the Roosevelt children's guardian in 1892, two years before their father's death.

ing and scolded her students for memorizing their lessons instead of using logic to figure them out. She was also deeply concerned with social is-

sues and politics. Eleanor became a favorite of the headmistress, who developed a motherly interest in her shy American student. Eleanor Roosevelt

Eleanor stands in the center of the back row in this photograph of the students at Allenswood, the London boarding school she attended from 1899 to 1902.

later remarked that "I felt that I was starting a new life, free from all my former sins and traditions . . . this was the first time in my life that my fears left me."

In February 1901 Souvestre took 16-year-old Eleanor on a trip to France and Italy, a journey that her young friend later referred to as "a revelation." Eleanor ate local cuisines, met artists and writers, and discovered whole new worlds she had never before imagined. In order to counteract the feelings of helplessness caused by her pupil's sheltered and unhappy childhood, Souvestre encouraged Elea-

nor to take care of the details of their trip. The headmistress also persuaded her to venture forth on her own during their stay in Florence, Italy. The joy Eleanor felt in exploring the art capital armed with only a guidebook came through in the description she wrote years later: "16 years old, keener than I have probably ever been and more alive to beauty, I sallied forth to see Florence alone."

At Allenswood, Eleanor blossomed intellectually, developing a passionate interest in her studies. Although she had been an avid reader since early childhood, her understanding of literature deepened during the course of her schooling. Her enthusiasm was apparent in an essay she wrote on the great English dramatist and poet William Shakespeare. She wrote that "He was not one man but a continent. He had in him great men, entire crowds, and landscapes."

She wanted desperately to return for a fourth year at Allenswood, but Grandmother Hall would not hear of it—she insisted that Eleanor come back home to make her official debut into New York society. For Eleanor this decision seemed a near tragedy. "I have spent three years here which have certainly been the happiest years of my life," she wrote before she left. Recalling her years with Marie Souvestre, she later said, "Whatever I have become since had its seeds in those three years of contact with a liberal mind and strong personality."

This portrait was taken in Switzerland in 1900. Marie Souvestre, Allenswood's headmistress, took Eleanor on trips across Europe to broaden the young woman's horizons.

Eleanor Roosevelt reluctantly left Allenswood in 1902 to make her debut in New York society. She attended parties and balls but felt ill at ease at these events.

THREE

Marriage and Motherhood

When Eleanor Roosevelt returned to the United States in the summer of 1902, she found the social and political climate of the nation revitalized, due in large part to her uncle Theodore. The youngest president America had yet elected, enthusiastic and optimistic, Teddy Roosevelt had captured the imagination of the country. Americans were fascinated not only by the politician but also by the private man and his family.

Unlike her flamboyant uncle, Eleanor Roosevelt was ill at ease when she appeared in public, a condition that was brought to the fore in December 1902, when the 18 year old made her debut into New York society at the posh Assembly Ball. According to her memoirs, she knew few people there and would have been virtually ignored were it not for two old family friends. "I

do not think I quite realized before-hand what utter agony it was going to be," she said of her debut, "or I would never have had the courage to go."

Determined not to disappoint her family, Roosevelt attended a dizzying array of parties during the social season of 1902–03, but she seldom enjoyed these events. She was uncomfortable making the light bantering conversation expected of young women, preferring to discuss the serious matters of the day, especially politics. An acquaintance from this period recalled, "She wasn't a belle by any means. She was too tall for most of the young men. But she was an interesting talker."

Roosevelt's interest in political matters was fostered by Anna Roosevelt Cowles, her father's sister. During Eleanor's visits to her aunt's house in

Eleanor's uncle, U.S. president Theodore Roosevelt, delivers an impassioned speech. He enjoyed widespread popularity during his years in office, 1901-09.

Washington, D.C., Cowles set an unforgettable example for her niece. Interesting and influential people frequently stopped by to discuss current events, and one of the most frequent callers was Cowles's brother, President Roosevelt. Young Eleanor sat mesmerized as her uncle consulted her aunt on affairs of state. "He may have made his own decisions," she remembered, "but talking with her seemed to clarify things for him." For the first time, Eleanor Roosevelt realized the influence a woman could wield—even indirectly—on policy-making.

Despite, or perhaps because of, her privileged background, Roosevelt felt compelled to work on behalf of the less fortunate. Anna Cowles and Marie Souvestre had both taught her that it was not enough to talk about society's problems; one must take an active part in alleviating them. Roosevelt joined the newly formed Junior League, a group of wealthy young women who helped New York City's poor. League volunteers worked in hospitals, or in settlement houses that assisted the immigrants who were flooding into America. Settlement-house workers often provided child care and lessons in such areas as sanitation and English. Roosevelt signed on to work at the Rivington Street Settlement House, located in the heart of the Lower East Side slums.

Working with impoverished children, women, and men was an awakening for Eleanor Roosevelt. Although she had always longed to be useful to others, never before had she come across so many who needed so much. The squalor in which some new immigrants lived left an indelible image in her mind, and she was determined to help in any way she could. Roosevelt taught immigrant children skills such as calisthenics, sewing, and dance. Because of her energy and dedication, she emerged as a leader in the Junior League. Her charitable activities did more than just help the poor and set an example for other young women; through her work, Eleanor Roosevelt was finding herself.

Strong convictions were driving Roosevelt to challenge herself in new ways. Many of the adults and children Roosevelt worked with at Rivington Street worked in sweatshops, factories that employed workers at low wages for long hours under poor conditions. Alarmed by the toll that these practices were taking on human lives, she volunteered to visit businesses and report on labor conditions for a reform organization called the Consumers' League. "I was frightened to death," Roosevelt reported later. "But this was what had been required of me and I wanted to be useful. I entered my first sweatshop.... I saw little children of four or five sitting at tables until they dropped with fatigue."

Her interest in politics and her dedication to helping the poor made her something of an outsider in her social set, but one prominent young man was intrigued by her intelligence and integrity. "Cousin Eleanor has a very good mind," Franklin Delano Roosevelt, Eleanor's distant cousin, remarked to his mother one day. The two of them had known one another since childhood, but now they began to meet at parties, horse shows, luncheons, and dances. Each time they were together it was apparent to those around them—if not to Eleanor Roosevelt—that her handsome cousin was beginning to care for her.

One Sunday in November 1903 FDR, as Franklin was nicknamed, accompanied Eleanor Roosevelt and her

As a volunteer for the Junior League, Eleanor Roosevelt worked to feed and educate impoverished New York City immigrant families such as the one pictured here.

brother Hall to Groton, the private school that Hall attended. During this visit Franklin asked Eleanor to marry him. "Why me?" she is reported to have responded. "I am plain. I have little to bring you." FDR disagreed wholeheartedly. Although he had few bright prospects at the moment, he told her that with her help he would some day amount to something.

History has borne out Franklin Roosevelt's conviction that Eleanor would be an asset to him, but at the time some thought that FDR was quite a "catch" for such an earnest, self-conscious young woman. In fact, marrying his distant cousin proved to be a fortunate personal and political move for FDR. Eleanor's cousin Alice Roosevelt Longworth expressed the idea that Eleanor may indeed have been more a "catch" than Franklin. "We used to say 'poor Franklin,'" she remarked. "The joke was on us."

Sara Delano Roosevelt, the future groom's mother, was disappointed by her son's romantic interest but was diplomatic enough to remain quiet about it. An iron-willed widow, she exerted considerable influence over her only child. Sara Roosevelt convinced the couple to keep their plans secret for a year. A long engagement, she told them, would give them time to examine their feelings. It seems likely,

A young girl works in a turn-of-the-century textile mill. Roosevelt inspected such factories for the Consumers' League and lobbied for laws restricting child labor.

however, that she was hoping their affections would cool over time.

Eleanor Roosevelt made a herculean effort to win over her future mother-in-law. While Franklin was finishing up at Harvard the two women spent many afternoons together having tea or going to the dressmaker's, but the rocky beginnings of their relationship were never smoothed out. Until the end of her life, Sara Delano Roosevelt would struggle to regain control over her son.

In the fall of 1904 Franklin entered Columbia Law School, and a few months later the couple finally announced their engagement. Eleanor Roosevelt's friend Muriel Robbins wrote her that "all those who know you think it is the luckiest thing that ever happened to Franklin." Franklin Roosevelt also received his share of congratulatory letters, among them one from Teddy Roosevelt, who had high hopes for the couple. "You and Eleanor are true and brave," the president wrote, "and I believe you love each other unselfishly; and golden years open before you."

One of Theodore Roosevelt's children reportedly quipped that "Father wants to be the bride at every wedding and the corpse at every funeral." Eleanor Roosevelt was the bride on March 17, 1905, but true to form, her uncle Teddy, who gave her away, stole the spotlight. Eleanor looked beautiful in her satin and lace wedding dress, but most of the spectators who gathered

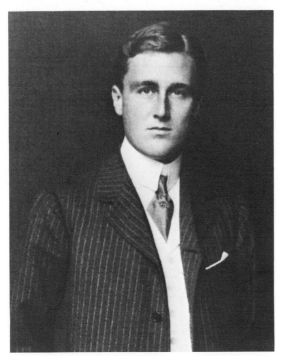

Franklin Delano Roosevelt is shown here in 1903, the year he and his distant cousin Eleanor became engaged.

moon until the school year ended. When summer came, the newlyweds sailed for Europe. Eleanor Roosevelt had been nervous about seasickness, but she was stalwart during the crossing. Her husband wrote his mother that "Eleanor has been a *wonderful* sailor and hasn't missed a single meal. Or," he mischievously added, "*lost* any either."

The couple enjoyed their honeymoon immensely. Their first stop was Liverpool, England, where they stayed

Eleanor Roosevelt converses with her future mother-in-law, Sara Delano Roosevelt. Intensely protective of her son, Sara disapproved of Franklin and Eleanor's relationship.

outside the Manhattan townhouse where the nuptials took place were more interested in catching a glimpse of the president. After the simple, elegant wedding ceremony, the exuberant Theodore Roosevelt congratulated the new groom. "Well, Franklin," he chuckled, "there's nothing like keeping the name in the family." The president then led the guests to the refreshment area, with Franklin and Eleanor Roosevelt trailing meekly behind.

Because Franklin Roosevelt was still in his first year of law school, the couple could not take their honey-

This picture of Eleanor and Franklin was taken during the couple's engagement, which they kept secret, at Sara Roosevelt's request, for more than a year.

Twenty-year-old Eleanor Roosevelt was a beautiful bride on her March 17, 1905 wedding day, but her flamboyant uncle, President Theodore Roosevelt, upstaged the newlyweds.

with relatives. In Paris, France, they shopped and visited the city's famed art museums; in Venice, Italy, they cruised the city's canals in a gondola. After climbing in the breathtaking Dolomite Alps, they went on to the ritzy Swiss vacation center of St. Moritz. While visiting friends in Scotland Eleanor was mortified when she was asked about the difference between America's state and federal governments and found she could not answer the question. She became determined to learn all she could about American government.

Although she had weathered the trip out beautifully, during the voyage home Eleanor Roosevelt was often violently ill. When the nausea continued even after she reached dry land, she visited her doctor and learned that she was pregnant. The newlyweds had another surprise in store for them when they came home: Sara Delano Roosevelt had rented them a house at 125 East 36th Street, two blocks from her own. She had already bought furniture and hired servants for them as well.

Because of Sara Roosevelt's meddling, Eleanor often felt like a guest in her own home, and as she grappled with the novel experience of caring for an infant, she grew dependent on her servants and mother-in-law. The Roosevelts' first child, Anna, was born on May 3, 1906. The first time the new mother held her daughter she was astonished by the connection she felt. To Eleanor Roosevelt, the baby was "just a helpless bundle, but by its mere helplessness winding itself inextricably around my heart." But Roosevelt was not only touched, she was frightened by her infant daughter's dependency, and she grew increasingly unsure of herself. She later described this difficult period in her memoirs: "I had high standards of what a wife and mother should be and not the faintest notion of what it meant to be either a wife or a mother."

Roosevelt's friend and biographer Joseph P. Lash characterized the first years of her marriage as a difficult time in which she lost much of the ground she had recently gained. "For five years before her marriage," he wrote, "she had begun to assert her individuality, sense her potentialities, and emerge as a tower of strength to those around her. Suddenly the pattern was reversed, and in return for the privilege of loving and being loved she stifled any impulse to assert herself."

While Franklin Roosevelt finished law school and began his legal career, his wife was at home giving birth to and raising their children. Eleanor

Eleanor and Franklin Roosevelt enjoy a quiet moment in the Italian countryside during their 1905 honeymoon.

Roosevelt later said of this time, "For ten years I was always just getting over having a baby or about to have one." In rapid successsion she gave birth to six children, five of whom survived infancy. James was born in 1907; Franklin, Jr., was born in 1909 but died of influenza before his first birthday; Elliott arrived in 1910; the second Franklin, Jr., was born in 1914; and the couple's last child, John, arrived in 1916.

The Roosevelts' family life settled into a routine. They spent most of the year in New York City, and summered on Campobello Island in New Bruns-

Franklin clowns for the camera. He and Eleanor were a handsome couple with bright prospects in 1906, the year this portrait was taken.

wick, Canada, where Franklin's family had vacationed for years. Even in the surroundings of this summer retreat, Eleanor Roosevelt was unable to unwind with the family she tried hard—often too hard—to please.

"Mother was always stiff," her daughter Anna remembered, "never relaxed enough to romp. Mother loved all mankind, but she did not know how to let her children love her." Roosevelt continued to withdraw from others, often falling prey to what she referred to as her "Griselda moods." During these gloomy states she felt herself, like patient Griselda in the writings of Geoffrey Chaucer, to be nothing more than a dutiful, resigned wife and mother.

In the autumn of 1908 the Roosevelts moved into a home built for them by Sara Roosevelt—a house that adjoined her own. On their first night in their new dwelling Franklin Roosevelt came home from work to find his wife sobbing. Although she had remained silent while the house was being planned, she was miserable at the prospect of living in a home that was more her mother-in-law's than her own. One of the worst problems with the new setup was the connecting doors that united the two households: "You were never quite sure when she would appear, day or night," Roosevelt later said of her mother-in-law.

Sara Delano Roosevelt interfered not only in Eleanor's relationship with her husband but in her relationship with her children as well. The older woman was fond of saying that Eleanor's children were really her own. "Your mother only bore you," she often told them. A young woman who had been raised to keep peace at all costs, Eleanor withdrew even further and ceded the field to her mother-in-law.

But although she was initially cowed by both her domineering mother-in-law and her ambitious and sometimes preoccupied husband, Eleanor Roosevelt would soon learn to stand on her own. "Perhaps," she later commented, "it was that having two such personalities as my husband and his mother, I had to develop willy-nilly into an individual myself."

Roosevelt cradles her newborn daughter, Anna, in 1906. Between 1906 and 1916, Eleanor and Franklin had six children, five of whom survived infancy.

Franklin Delano Roosevelt campaigns for the New York state senate in 1910, launching a political career that closely mirrored his distant cousin Teddy Roosevelt's.

FOUR

Entering Public Life

Franklin Roosevelt envisioned a bright career ahead of him. He planned to follow almost exactly in Theodore Roosevelt's footsteps: He would be elected to the state legislature, be appointed assistant secretary of the navy, win the governorship of New York, and, he hoped, move on to the presidency. Eleanor fully supported Franklin's ambitions and was prepared to make sacrifices so that he could achieve them. Although her immediate family, including her beloved uncle Teddy, had always been Republican, she switched her allegiance to her husband's political group, the Democratic party.

Just as he had hoped, in 1910 Franklin Roosevelt won a seat in the New York state legislature as the representative from Dutchess County, where his family's Hyde Park estate was lo-

cated. His new office made it necessary for the family to move to the state capital. On New Year's Day, 1911, the Roosevelts moved into a three-story brownstone in Albany. The move marked the beginning of a new era for Eleanor Roosevelt, now 26 years old.

Finally away from the overbearing Sara Delano Roosevelt, she was delighted to find that she could manage on her own. Of that time she later wrote, "I had to stand on my feet now, and I think it was good for me." She continued, "I was beginning to realize that something within me craved to be an individual."

For Eleanor Roosevelt, the process of becoming an individual was a gradual one. She began by taking part in her husband's career. As she wrote in her memoirs, she felt that "it was a wife's duty to be interested in whatever in-

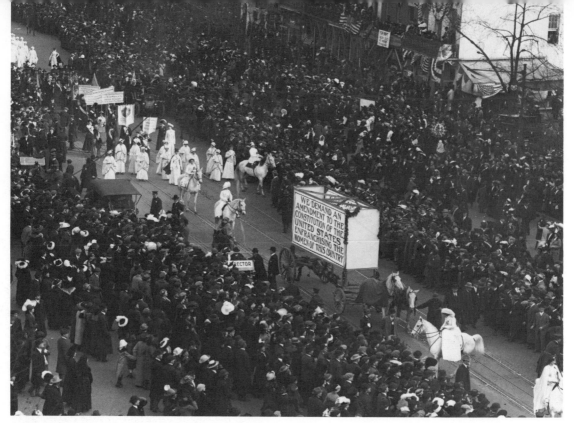

Suffragists take to the streets of Washington, D.C., in 1913 to demand women's right to vote. Initially skeptical, Eleanor was pleased when women won the vote in 1920.

terested her husband, whether it was politics, books or a dish for dinner." She began to read about public affairs and to sit in on state assembly meetings. In 1912 she attended her first Democratic party convention. Despite these activities, she thought of herself first and foremost as the wife of a public official. "I took an interest in politics," she recalled later, "but don't know whether I enjoyed it."

A group of men, primarily FDR's associates in the Democratic party, came by the Roosevelt's Albany home nearly every night to engage in lively discussions. They met in the library, but Eleanor Roosevelt, acting the role

of retiring wife, usually sat by herself in the living room, knitting. One by one, however, FDR's colleagues discovered that the new senator's quiet spouse possessed a lively intelligence and would seek her out to chat. One of those who appreciated Roosevelt's special qualities was Louis Howe, a newspaper reporter who would serve as her husband's right-hand man throughout most of FDR's political career.

Soon after entering politics, State Senator Franklin Roosevelt embarked on a difficult fight against Tammany Hall. This organization was a powerful political group that had influenced

New York Democratic politics since 1789. By daring to ignore the dictates of this organization, Roosevelt was earning a reputation as a maverick, and began to receive a great deal of press coverage.

As a prominent politician's wife, Eleanor Roosevelt also received a good deal of attention, much of which made her uncomfortable. This modest fame, however, brought Eleanor her first fan letter, which she kept for many years. "I know very well," wrote a stranger, "[Franklin] never could do so well, and be so brave, if he were not upheld and strengthened in every way by his wife."

During this period, the only role that Eleanor Roosevelt envisioned for women in public service was that of politician's wife. She "took it for granted," she recalled, "that men were superior creatures and knew more about politics than women." She was still very much a product of her conservative upbringing and believed that women did not even deserve the right to vote. Her husband, however, supported a proposed constitutional amendment that would extend the ballot to women.

Franklin Roosevelt realized another of his career goals when he was appointed assistant secretary of the navy in 1913. The family moved to the nation's capital, where they sublet Anna Cowles's residence, the house that had been called "the little White House" during Teddy Roosevelt's administra-

Assistant Secretary of the Navy Franklin Roosevelt confers with two high-ranking officers. The Roosevelts moved to Washington in 1913 when FDR won his appointment.

tion. The former president wrote FDR, "It is interesting to see that you are in another place which I myself once held."

Eleanor Roosevelt's schedule was often as busy as her husband's. She dutifully began to make inroads into Washington society, spending hours on the exhausting task of "visiting." "I've paid 60 calls in Washington this week and have been to a luncheon at the Marine barracks," she wrote at the end of one long day. "We've been out to dinner every night, last night a big

Announcing that "the world must be made safe for democracy," President Woodrow Wilson asks Congress to declare war on Germany. The United States entered World War I in April 1917.

Navy League affair for Mr. Daniels [the secretary of the navy] where there was some really good speaking."

She was soon to hear "speaking" that would change the lives of millions of Americans. On a gloomy April morning in 1917 President Woodrow Wilson summoned the U.S. Congress "to receive a communication concerning grave matters." Eleanor Roosevelt attended the special session and heard the president explain that the United States could no longer remain a by-stander in the war that had engaged most of Europe since 1914. "The world," he announced, "must be made safe for democracy." "I went and listened breathlessly," Roosevelt reported later, "and returned home still half-dazed by the sense of impending change."

As soldiers packed transport ships headed for the battlefields of Europe, American women toiled on the home front. Many left the domestic sphere behind to take an active part in the war effort, and Roosevelt was among their ranks. As biographer Joseph Lash noted, "The war gave her a reason acceptable to her conscience to free herself of the social duties that she hated, to concentrate less on her household, and to plunge into work that fitted her aptitudes."

She devoted herself to volunteer work, knitting scarves, sweaters, and socks for servicemen and mobilizing other women to do the same. She cofounded the Navy Relief Society and served meals to hungry soldiers passing through Washington's Union Station. She also joined the Red Cross canteen, where she took over accounting responsibilities.

The war in Europe meant shortages and sacrifices at home, so Roosevelt experimented with measures that would enable her to economize. When her domestic system was selected by the *New York Times* "as a model for other large households," she got her first taste of the perils of dealing with the press. The *Times* quoted her as saying: "Making ten servants help me do my saving has not only been possible but highly profitable." Realizing how callous and insensitive her out-ofcontext quote made her sound, Roosevelt was mortified: "I feel dreadfully about it, because so much is not true, and yet some of it I did say. I never will be caught again, that's sure, and I'd like to crawl away for shame." FDR, however, laughed the matter off. "All I can say," he wrote his wife, "is that your latest newspaper campaign is a corker and I am proud to be the husband of the Originator, Discoverer, and Inventor of the New Household Economy for Millionaires!"

Eleanor Roosevelt's volunteer activities included inspecting hospitals for the Red Cross. One of these visits brought her to St. Elizabeth's Hospital, a Washington institution that treated mentally ill individuals, many of whom had suffered breakdowns on the World War I battlefields. "The first time I went to the ward," Roosevelt reported, "I wanted to bang at the door to get out. But I was ashamed of myself. I would not have shown my terror for the world." Roosevelt's repressed terror soon gave way to concern for the patients at the understaffed hospital, who had, she noted, "apparently very little attention paid them." She asked Secretary of the Interior Frank Lane to investigate St. Elizabeth's, and, as a result, the government increased the institution's funding.

Roosevelt's daunting array of wartime activities left her exhausted, but she could never say no to a good cause. "I begin to feel," an overworked Roosevelt complained during this period, "that only a hermit's life will ever give me joy again." But her reawakened political and social convictions would not allow her to lead a hermit's existence or even return to the exclusively family-oriented life she led before the war. As Joseph Lash noted, "She would never again be content with purely private satisfactions, and for the rest of her life she would look at the injustice of the world, feel pity for the human condition, and ask what she could do about it."

The hardships faced by millions in the United States and Europe diminished as World War I drew to a close in the autumn of 1918, but Eleanor Roosevelt faced a personal sorrow during

Volunteers solicit funds for the Red Cross during World War I. Roosevelt was a member of this organization, which cared for soldiers and provided war relief for civilians.

Women toil at a paper mill during World War I. Like thousands of other American women, Roosevelt put aside domestic tasks to help the war effort.

this period. In September Franklin came down with double pneumonia. Because he was confined to his bed, she took on the responsibility of handling his mail. In this way she happened upon love letters from Lucy Mercer, an attractive young woman who served as Eleanor's social secretary. Though she had long suspected something between her flirtatious husband and Mercer, she was shocked when she found out about the affair. She offered Franklin a divorce, but he refused, both because he knew that it would do untold damage to his political career and also because Mercer's

Catholicism prohibited her from marrying a divorced man. Eleanor stayed in the marriage out of a sense of obligation to her children, and also because her loyalty to her husband was largely undiminished by his infidelity.

Although Franklin Roosevelt tried his best to make amends, the Lucy Mercer episode was devastating to his wife. "The bottom dropped out of my own particular world and I faced myself, my surroundings, my world, honestly for the first time. I really grew up that year," she wrote later. She had put all her trust and hopes in Franklin, and he had let her down profoundly, reinforcing all the insecurities of her youth. Feeling that she could no longer rely on him as she once had, she resolved to stop living her life through her husband. "Somewhere along the line of development," she said years later, "we discover what we really are, and then we make our real decisions for which we are responsible. Make that decision primarily for yourself because you can never really live anyone else's life."

As Eleanor Roosevelt reevaluated her personal goals and her marriage, Franklin's career continued to prosper. In 1920 Democratic presidential candidate James M. Cox asked FDR to run for the vice-presidential slot. Campaigning across the country with her husband, Roosevelt began a close friendship with Louis Howe, now one of FDR's closest advisers. Knowing that she would be an asset to the Democratic ticket, Howe enlisted her aid. The two of them made a formidable team. He coached her on politics; she advised him on how to handle her husband. Before long, Roosevelt was assisting Howe with speech writing and managing the campaign. It was the beginning of an enduring partnership. Of Howe, Joseph Lash wrote: "Long ago he had set his hand to making a king; now he began to make a queen."

Just as she had eventually come to love politics, Eleanor Roosevelt had also come around on another front, woman suffrage. The 1920 election was

In September 1918 Eleanor learned of FDR's affair with her social secretary Lucy Mercer (pictured above). He promised to end the relationship but eventually resumed it.

the first in which American women could vote, and she did all she could to encourage them to exercise that right. But despite vigorous campaigning, the Cox-Roosevelt ticket was defeated, and FDR joined a prestigious New York law firm later known as Emmett, Marvin, and Roosevelt.

For her part, Eleanor Roosevelt may have left Washington, but she did not give up on politics. She joined the League of Women Voters, a group that was founded in 1920 to help newly enfranchised women make intelligent use of their voting privileges. She was asked to keep track of legislation on

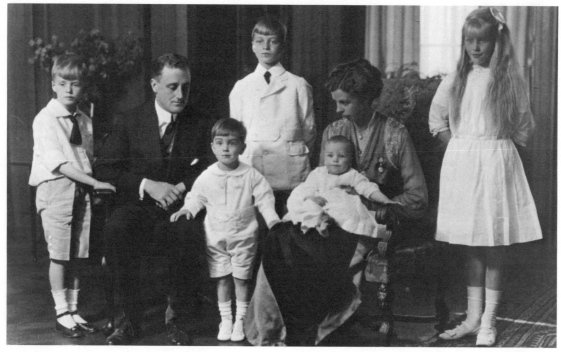

Although she was devastated by FDR's affair with Lucy Mercer, Eleanor stayed with him, in part because of their five children.

such issues as labor reform, the rights of children, and international peace.

Roosevelt grew a great deal as a result of her association with the League of Women Voters. She served as a delegate to state and national league conventions, where, for the first time in her life, she gave public speeches. Her no-nonsense activism impressed her colleagues. A friend from this period, Esther Lape, remarked that, "The rest of us were inclined to do a good deal of theorizing. She would look puzzled and asked why we didn't do whatever we had in mind and get it out of the way."

The Roosevelt family spent the summer of 1921 at their retreat on Campobello Island, but instead of the rest that they hoped for, they experienced a major setback. On August 10 FDR began to complain of chills and fatigue; a few days later he was paralyzed from the chest down. After several weeks, Franklin's puzzling illness was finally diagnosed as poliomyelitis, a paralyzing disease usually referred to as polio. The doctors told Eleanor and Franklin that he might recover some use of his legs after a long stint of physical therapy, but they held out no hope for complete recovery. Franklin Roosevelt's spirit was indomitable, however, and he insisted that he would walk again. He eventually did—but only with the help of heavy metal leg braces. Eleanor supported her husband's courageous efforts to recover and told Franklin's doctor, "If you relegate my husband to the wheelchair now, and forbid him the interests he needs to stimulate his mind, you will be making him an invalid for life. If he fights, he may overcome his handicap."

When it became clear that FDR would not be able to return to public life for some time, Louis Howe asked Eleanor keep the Roosevelt name in the public eye. A woman who had been a staunch Republican until her marriage, she emerged as one of the Democratic party's most impassioned supporters. With Louis Howe's help, she edited the *Women's Democratic News*, and she often volunteered at the New York State Democratic headquarters, where she took on tasks ranging from licking stamps to fund-raising. As a novice speaker, Roosevelt tended to lose her voice or giggle nervously when addressing large groups. Howe's advice was simple and to the point: "Have something to say, say it, and then sit down." Roosevelt followed his sugges-

James M. Cox and Franklin Roosevelt parade through the streets of Dayton, Ohio, in 1920 after the Democratic party nominated them for president and vice-president.

tion, and many years later she would give the same advice to those she took under her protective wing.

During this period Roosevelt wrote an eloquent article for the Junior League *Bulletin* entitled "Why I Am a Democrat." This piece expressed her belief that the Democratic party gave a higher priority to human needs than the Republican party did. "On the whole," she wrote, "the Democratic party seems to have been more concerned with the welfare and interests of the people at large, and less with the growth of big business."

"Why I Am a Democrat" also summed up Roosevelt's rejection of the aristocratic values of her youth. All her life she had felt for those less fortunate than she, but her motivation seems to have been *noblesse oblige*, that is, the notion that society's wealthy have an obligation to help the poor. She still held this belief, but she now felt that advantages such as education and prosperity should be more

Advisers Louis Howe (far left) and Tom Lynch confer with the Roosevelts during FDR's unsuccessful bid for the vice-presidency. Howe considered Eleanor a valuable political asset.

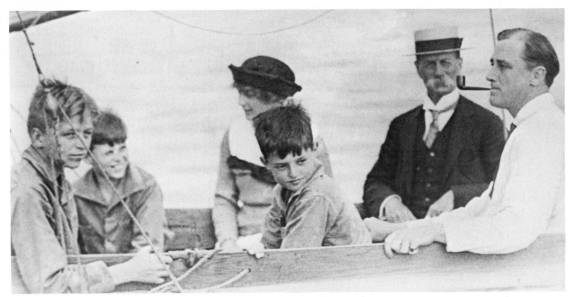

A pipe-smoking FDR takes his family out for a sail in 1920. The following year he came down with polio, a disease that left him partially paralyzed.

equally distributed within society, not merely left to the upper classes to dole out to the poor as they saw fit. She summarized her view in her article: "If you believe that a nation is really better off which achieves for a comparative few, those who are capable of attaining it, high culture, ease, opportunity and that these few from their enlightenment should give what they consider best to those less favored, then you naturally belong to the Republican party." Anyone who believed otherwise, who believed that all individuals should have equal opportunities to "struggle slowly to the light for themselves" must, in Roosevelt's mind, be a Democrat.

Her truly democratic spirit drew her into the Women's Trade Union League (WTUL), founded by social worker Jane Addams and other progressive women in 1903 "to aid women workers in their efforts to organize and to secure better conditions." It was a militant organization, and many of its members were outspoken feminists. In her work for the group, she pushed for such reforms as the 40-hour work week, the abolition of child labor, minimum wages, and the right to organize unions.

In 1924 Roosevelt wrote her convalescing husband that "I'm only being active till you can be again—it isn't such a great desire on my part to serve the world and I'll fall back into habits of sloth quite easily!" But to all who knew her, these self-effacing words would not have rung true. It was clear that her views and aspirations were continually expanding—and that Eleanor Roosevelt had become a force to be reckoned with.

Roosevelt and Nancy Cook (center) consult with a carpenter at Val-Kill Industries. The two women started the business along with their friend Marion Dickerman.

FIVE

The First Lady of New York

Eleanor Roosevelt's advice to women interested in entering politics was simple yet adamant: "Get into the game and stay in it. Throwing mud from the outside won't help. Building up from the inside will." Taking her own advice, she took on the power brokers at the 1924 Democratic State Convention. An all-male group of politicians had insisted that they, not the Women's Division of the New York Democratic Committee, should choose the convention's female delegates. A member of the women's committee, Roosevelt took up the battle standard.

"Women," she maintained, "must gain for themselves a place of real equality and the respect of the men," a goal that could only be achieved by working "with" men, rather than merely "for" them. "To many women, and I am one of them," she continued,

"it is extraordinarily difficult to care about anything enough to cause disagreement or unpleasant feelings, but I have come to the conclusion that this must be done for a time until we can prove our strength and demand respect for our wishes." Roosevelt's outspoken stand captured press attention and swayed New York governor Alfred E. Smith, and the state party establishment finally agreed to allow the women's committee to select delegates. Two years later, Roosevelt and her allies won another victory when women began to be elected to the Democratic State Committee on an individual basis, not as part of a Women's Division.

Along with two friends, Democratic party activists Nancy Cook and Marion Dickerman, Roosevelt also started a small furniture manufacturing busi-

FDR reads of his victory in the 1928 race for the New York governor's seat. The contest marked his reentrance into politics after his crippling bout with polio.

ness in Hyde Park during this period. The venture began when Eleanor, who had never felt at home at the family estate dominated by Sara Delano Roosevelt, convinced her husband to finance the construction of a cottage for herself and her friends. The cozy stone house, named Val-Kill after a nearby stream, became a beloved retreat for Eleanor, and Cook and Dickerman lived there most of the year. At Val-Kill the three women functioned as a kind of family—the sheets and towels even bore the monogram "EMN."

Cook, who had once taught woodworking, built furniture for the cottage. The pieces turned out so well that Cook, Dickerman, and Roosevelt opened Val-Kill Industries to produce more of it. Cook handled the manufacturing side while Roosevelt promoted, publicized, and managed the business. One of the primary motives behind the project was providing employment for the impoverished local population.

Once Val-Kill Industries was running smoothly, the three women embarked on a new project. Dickerman was vice-principal of New York City's Todhunter School, a private institution for girls. When the school went up for sale in 1927, the three women decided to take it over. Eleanor Roosevelt served as the school's vice principal and taught literature, drama, and American history.

Like her beloved mentor, Marie Souvestre, Roosevelt required her students to examine both the world around

Eleanor Roosevelt (front row, second from right) enjoys a Todhunter School outing. Roosevelt began teaching history and literature at the girls' school in 1927.

them and their own personal beliefs. Her exams included essay topics such as "How are Negroes excluded from voting in the South?" and "Give your reason for or against allowing women to actively participate in the control of government . . . as well as your reasons for or against women holding office in the government." In her current events course, called "Happenings," Roosevelt encouraged her students to take part in activities outside their protected sphere. She took these well-heeled young women to impoverished areas of the city so that they could see what she herself had seen at their age. She taught, she inspired, and she enjoyed herself thoroughly. As Marion Dickerman commented, "Teaching gave her some of the happiest mo-

ments in her life. She loved it. The girls worshipped her."

Although she continued her work at Todhunter and Val-Kill, Democratic party politics became a primary concern for Eleanor Roosevelt as the 1928 elections approached. FDR had recuperated from his illness enough to run for governor of New York that year. Eleanor supported her husband's bid, but she focused most of her energy on working for the man who had just vacated the governor's post, presidential candidate Al Smith. As the head of the Women's Committee for Al Smith she traveled extensively, even to remote rural areas, delivering straightforward, idealistic speeches she had written herself. Her orations emphasized Smith's work as a humanitarian

Eleanor Roosevelt boards a plane in 1930. Because FDR had difficulty walking, she often served as his "legs," traveling across the state to report on local conditions.

who had instituted welfare legislation in the areas of health care, housing, farm relief, and education. Speaking one year before the stock market crash that would devastate much of the world's economy, she announced prophetically, "We do not want an economy which refuses to help those who need and deserve the help of the state, nor do we want the kind of economy which saves a little today and loses much opportunity for the future."

Roosevelt was disappointed when Smith lost the presidential contest to Republican Herbert Hoover, who would pursue the kind of "hands-off" economic policies that she opposed. FDR, however, had won the gubernatorial election, and the family moved back to Albany. One of Eleanor Roosevelt's first acts in her new role was to create a dining and living room for the servants living in the governor's mansion, whom she felt were not being treated properly. She also made it very clear that she had no intention of abandoning her teaching career, and spent three days each week at Todhunter. "I teach because I love it," she said firmly. "I cannot give it up."

As the first lady of New York Eleanor Roosevelt was in an excellent position to effect political change. She worked to promote reform and to help women break into politics, exerting her influence subtly and judiciously. "I hope you will consider making [labor activist and public official] Frances Perkins Labor Commissioner," she wrote her husband soon after his victory, "and put Nell Schwartz (now head of the Bureau of Women in Industry) on the Commission so there would be one woman on it." She diplomatically hastened to add, "These are suggestions which I'm passing on, not my opinions for I don't mean to butt in." The governor did, eventually, appoint Frances Perkins and Nell Schwartz to the positions suggested by his wife.

As governor it was important for Franklin Roosevelt to visit state institutions and conduct on-site inspections. But his wheelchair made this difficult. Instead, he often drove around the grounds talking with the state officials, sending Eleanor inside to look over hospitals, prisons, and government offices. FDR found her first reports too vague, but she soon learned what to look for. "It was he," Eleanor Roosevelt said of her husband, "who taught me to observe. Just sitting with him in the observation car of a train I learned how

to watch the tracks and see their condition, how to look at the countryside and note whether there was soil erosion, and what condition the forest and fields were in."

Although they shared a keen interest in politics and the welfare of the American people, Franklin and Eleanor Roosevelt were leading fairly separate lives as the 1920s drew to a close. They were often apart for weeks at a time, and love seemed to give way to mutual respect. As their son James later commented, after the Lucy Mercer affair "father and mother had an armed truce that endured until the day he died." In their son's opinion, Franklin and Eleanor viewed each other "as

Roosevelt greets well-wishers during her first day at the governor's mansion in Albany. During FDR's two terms as governor, she pursued both official and independent projects.

business partners, not as husband and wife."

In October 1929 the stock market crashed, setting off a period of world-wide economic turmoil known as the Great Depression. Banks and businesses failed, farmers lost their land, workers lost their jobs, and millions of Americans were deprived of their

Although she campaigned for FDR, Eleanor Roosevelt had mixed feelings when he won the presidency in 1932. She feared that the role of first lady would restrict her to ceremonial duties.

A victim of the economic collapse known as the Great Depression stands in front of his makeshift dwelling. The depression began with the stock market crash of 1929.

homes and all sense of financial security. At the height of the depression, more than 12 million U.S. citizens were unemployed. It was a time of riots and breadlines. A song from the period immortalized the question asked by many destitute Americans: "Brother, Can You Spare a Dime?"

Campaigning in this volatile economic and political climate was rough, but in 1932 Franklin Roosevelt decided to run for the presidency on a reform platform. With such slogans as Abolish breadlines: Vote for Roosevelt, FDR appealed to the country's struggling population. Some of his most ardent support came from women organized or inspired by his wife, who often worked with a group affectionately called the grass-trampers. These women went from door to door praising FDR and distributing flyers designed by Eleanor that outlined the candidate's positions on key issues. Eleanor Roosevelt also traveled extensively, making speeches, mostly to women, about the future that she and her husband envisioned for the nation. "We must reorganize our economic structure," she told her listeners, "so that it may be possible for those willing to work to receive adequate compensation."

Eleanor Roosevelt was daunted not by the presidential race but by the prospect of winning it. She disliked the idea of leaving behind the friends and work she had established in New York. More than anything, she dreaded becoming first lady, traditionally a largely ceremonial role that revolved around the observance of protocol. But for her husband's sake—and, she believed, the good of the country—she hid her emotions. She wrote in her memoir *This I Remember* that "it was pure selfishness on my part, and I never mentioned my feelings on the subject to him."

In November 1932 Franklin Roosevelt won a landslide victory over Re-

FDR (far right) campaigned for the presidency in 1932 by promising a "new deal" for Americans suffering through the Great Depression.

publican incumbent Herbert Hoover. When the press asked for Eleanor's comment, her response was measured: "You're always pleased to have someone you're very devoted to have what he wants." But while others celebrated, Eleanor Roosevelt soberly considered the future. America's new first lady told the press that "it's an extremely serious thing to undertake, you know, the guidance of a nation at a time like this. It's not something you just laugh off and say you're pleased about."

In many ways, Eleanor Roosevelt probably wished that she could just "laugh off" the demands of her new role. "I never wanted to be a President's wife," she confided to a friend, newspaper reporter Lorena Hickok, shortly after the election, "and I don't want it now."

The Roosevelts salute the crowd after FDR's third presidential inauguration. When she arrived at the White House in 1933, Eleanor did not suspect that she would live there for 12 years.

SIX

To the White House

Franklin Roosevelt had pledged to give Americans a "new deal" after the rotten economic luck they had weathered during the past few years. During his campaign, he had made promises and offered reassurances, and millions of people had come to trust him and look to him for guidance. In his inspirational 1933 inaugural address, FDR assured his constituents that their faith was not misplaced. "The only thing we have to fear," he announced, "is fear itself." He continued, "This nation asks for action, and action now. Our greatest primary task is to put people to work."

Franklin Roosevelt brought with him to Washington not only a New Deal but a new kind of first lady. Although Eleanor Roosevelt had been afraid that her official responsibilities would force her to curtail her independent projects, she managed instead to adapt the role of first lady to her personality. The difference between Roosevelt and her predecessors was apparent right from the start. Invited by Mrs. Hoover to tour the White House before moving in, she declined the presidential car offered her, and opted, to the surprise of all, to walk over instead. When Roosevelt asked Lou Hoover what she regretted most about leaving the White House, Hoover replied that she would miss being taken care of.

Eleanor Roosevelt, by contrast, preferred to take care of things herself. When she and her family came to Washington, she moved furniture because she could not be bothered to wait for someone to help her. Breaking protocol, she declared that she would operate the White House elevator herself. She vowed that Americans would

Escorted by the chief usher, Eleanor Roosevelt, the wife of the president-elect, leaves the White House after a January 1933 visit to her future home.

Roosevelt gives a radio address in 1934. Unlike any first lady before her, she kept in constant touch with Americans via newspapers, magazines, and radio.

no longer have a first lady who was little more than a symbol of elegance. Instead, she insisted, "there is just going to be plain, ordinary Mrs. Roosevelt." But her very "ordinariness" would make her an extraordinary first lady.

To the delight of the American people—and to the dismay of Washington society—Eleanor Roosevelt set about democratizing the White House. Soon the president's dwelling was dubbed "Hull House on Pennsylvania Avenue," after Jane Addams's famous Chicago settlement house. By setting up scores

of informal meetings, the Roosevelts opened the doors of America's most revered mansion to all: young and old, white and black, rich and poor. Eleanor was proud that millions of Americans felt a kinship with her husband and his administration. In her opinion, "the feeling that in the house where government resides, there also resides a friendship, is perhaps the greatest safeguard we have for democracy."

Two days before her husband's first presidential press conference, Roosevelt set a precedent by becoming the first U.S. leader's wife to hold one

Roosevelt meets with newswomen. To encourage the employment of women in journalism, her precedent-setting press conferences were limited to female correspondents.

herself. In order to encourage newspapers to hire more women reporters, her press conferences, which became regular events, were open only to female correspondents. In deference to tradition, she tried to steer clear of politics at these meetings, but she spoke out on a wide range of social issues.

Roosevelt realized that communication was essential if she and FDR were to understand, and be understood by, the American people. Accordingly, she began a monthly column for *Women's Home Companion* magazine and she asked her readers to write in about

their concerns and hopes. Write her they did—during her first year in the White House, she received more than 300,000 pieces of mail. She also began giving radio talks, and she continued on the lecture circuit.

Although she had begun as an awkward and somewhat reluctant speaker, she eventually developed into an unflappable orator. Her ability to calmly adapt to a crisis was demonstrated one evening at Oak Park Junior College in Illinois. She had prepared a speech on "Peace," a topic selected by the school's administration. But during her introduction, the chair of the meeting announced that "Mrs. Roosevelt will speak on 'A Citizen's Responsibility to the Community.'" Scarcely missing a beat, Roosevelt delivered an impromptu address on the new subject.

As time passed, she also became more adept at handling difficult or embarrassing questions. In the style of a true politician, she often managed to turn the tables on her questioner in order to make a point of her own. Roosevelt displayed this skill during an exchange in Akron, Ohio, when a woman asked, "Do you think your husband's illness has affected your husband's mentality?" Although she probably considered this inquiry rude, her listeners could not tell from her response. "I am glad that question was asked," she replied. "The answer is yes. Anyone who has gone through great suffering is bound to have a greater sympathy and understanding of the problems of mankind."

Although she curtailed some of her overtly political activities when she became first lady, Roosevelt affected government policy through her considerable influence over her husband. Sometimes her attempts were subtle. For example, if someone approached

The first lady boards a coal train in 1935 to inspect an Ohio mine. She traveled across the country to check on public welfare and the effectiveness of government programs.

her about a cause to which she was sympathetic, she might arrange to have that person sit next to the president at dinner so that FDR would hear about it. In other instances, her involvement was direct and unapologetic. Columnist Raymond Clapper called her "a Cabinet Minister without portfolio—the most influential woman of our time." And government official Rexford Tugwell noted that

This photo shows one of the homes built at Arthurdale. Roosevelt helped plan this government-funded community, established to help the unemployed reach self-sufficiency.

> no one who ever saw Eleanor Roosevelt sit down facing her husband, and, holding his eye firmly, say to him "Franklin, I think you should" . . . or "Franklin, surely you will not" . . . will ever forget the experience. . . . It would be impossible to say how often and to what extent American governmental processes have been turned in a new direction because of her determination that people should be hurt as little as possible and that as much should be done for them as could be managed; the whole, if it could be totalled, would be formidable.

One of the tasks she took on as first lady was traveling across the country to report on how Americans were weathering the Great Depression. She visited city slums and impoverished farming communities and reported on the progress of government employment and relief programs. At the end of each long day on the road, she typed up reports for her husband or worked on articles for newspapers and magazines. To a nation accustomed to seeing a first lady do little more than look on raptly as her husband ad-

dressed his constituents, Eleanor Roosevelt was a revelation. And to a nation gripped by a devastating economic crisis, her concern and assurances provided comfort and hope.

Roosevelt was active in a number of projects aimed at alleviating the ill effects of the Great Depression. One of them was the Arthurdale Resettlement Administration Project, a plan to create a model community to aid the coal miners of West Virginia. Government officials hoped that Arthurdale would be the first of many communities where previously unemployed people would farm small plots and work in nearby factories. FDR's administration constructed homes for 150 families to purchase over time.

Roosevelt observes Works Progress Administration (WPA) workers in Georgia. The WPA provided employment for millions of jobless Americans, from laborers to artists.

As biographer Tamara K. Hareven pointed out in *Eleanor Roosevelt: An American Conscience*, the first lady was drawn to the project because "she saw in homestead communities a promise of human dignity for people who had been hopelessly destitute." Roosevelt established a school near Arthurdale, a handicraft project to employ local workers, and a clinic—the only health facility in the county. Roosevelt felt a personal connection with the families she was helping to escape from poverty. Many of the residents of Arthurdale came to know the first lady during her visits there and confided their hopes and frustrations to her.

Despite the good intentions and hard work of many committed people, the project foundered. Government representatives hoped to create jobs for the miners by enticing private industry into the area, but they were unable to do so. The attitude of the miners themselves was another problem at Arthurdale. Families who had struggled to survive poverty were wary of participating in projects that required them, for example, to donate part of their harvest to school lunch programs. "The homesteaders who were moved into the model community had been wary of the project from the start," Eleanor Roosevelt later said. "They trusted nobody, not even themselves. They had an eye out all the time to see who was going to cheat them next."

Although Arthurdale failed to develop into the self-supporting community Roosevelt and her co-workers had envisioned, she never regretted the experiment. Even when the Arthurdale project came under increasing fire from the press, she defended it vigorously. Like some other New Deal programs in which the government intervened to stimulate the economy, the program drew charges that it was a stepping stone to a communist state. Responding to these charges, Roosevelt announced at a press conference that "Never in this country to my knowledge has it been considered communistic for an opportunity to be given to people to earn their own livings and buy their own houses." The Arthurdale project failed to wipe out unemployment in the area, but the school and the clinic proved to be lasting institutions that changed the lives of many of the region's residents. The Arthurdale experiment eventually inspired FDR's administration to create 33 other such communities.

Eleanor Roosevelt was active in many other New Deal programs, the primary purpose of all being to help the poor and rejuvenate the U.S. economy. She took an active interest in the National Recovery Administration (NRA), where she lobbied for consumer rights and equal pay for women. Officials at another New Deal agency, the Agricultural Adjustment Administration (AAA), were swayed by her strong powers of persuasion to route surplus farm goods to the hungry. Working with Harry Hopkins, the administrator of the Civil Works Administration (CWA), she helped to create projects

Protesters stage a dramatic 1934 vigil in Washington, D.C., to urge legislators to pass a federal antilynching law. Eleanor Roosevelt lobbied for the bill.

The first lady talks to a child in a Detroit, Michigan, slum. Roosevelt was one of black America's most stalwart and influential champions in the 1930s and 1940s.

for the unemployed, particularly women and young people. When that program was superseded by the Works Progress Administration (WPA), she saw to it that unemployed artists—actors, writers, painters, and musicians—were also included.

Life magazine called another new government bureau, the National Youth Administration (NYA), Eleanor Roosevelt's "pet government agency." The NYA was set up to provide full-time jobs for young people, and to give part-time jobs to high school and college students so that they could afford to continue their education. From the very beginning of the program in 1935,

Roosevelt wanted to be sure that black youths would be part of the project. Accordingly, she asked Mary McLeod Bethune, the founder of Bethune-Cookman College, a black college in Florida, to join the NYA's advisory board.

Eleanor Roosevelt was passionately concerned with equal rights, and black Americans quickly discovered that they had a friend in the first lady. She invited many blacks, from political leaders to sharecroppers, to the White House to discuss what could be done to promote civil rights. She also spoke on racial issues at forums around the country. When Roosevelt addressed white audiences, she attempted to educate them about the injustice and danger of racism. She joined her moral arguments to pragmatic warnings: "If we have to put it on a self-interest basis," she said, then racism must end "for the preservation of the best that is in the ideals of this country, because you can have no part of the population beaten down and expect the rest of the country not to feel the effects from the big groups that are underprivileged." When Roosevelt spoke to black audiences, she emphasized the importance of education and organization. She recognized that, like women, blacks needed to produce leaders who could "qualify as the best in any field of endeavor" in order to combat prejudice.

Roosevelt's convictions were tested

in 1935, when she traveled to Birmingham, Alabama, for a meeting on social and political reforms. There were many black delegates to the conference, but because of the city's rigidly enforced segregation ordinance, they were forced to sit together on one side of the room. Roosevelt arrived with her ally in the civil rights struggle, Mary McLeod Bethune and had every intention of sitting next to her black friend. When the police instructed her that by doing so she was breaking the law, she refused to move to the "white" side of the room and instead placed her chair in the middle of the aisle separating the races. In this way Roosevelt compromised with the authorities without abandoning her principles.

Because of these same principles, Roosevelt was a supporter of the National Association for the Advancement of Colored People (NAACP), a group founded in 1909 to secure equal political, educational, and civil rights for blacks. During the 1920s and 1930s, the NAACP focused a great deal of effort on passing a national antilynching bill. Lynching, or execution without a lawful trial, was a relatively common practice in the 19th and early 20th centuries. Between 1889 and 1918, 3,224 people were lynched in the United States—more than 2,500 of them black. Many of these victims were wrongly accused, or not even suspected of serious crimes. Instead, lynching was often used as a violent

outlet for racial hatred. The ravages of the Great Depression spawned a revival of the practice as frightened, angry mobs turned men and women into scapegoats. In 1933 there were 28 lynchings; 24 of the victims were black. When the NAACP sponsored a New York City exhibition of artwork depicting the horrors of these murders, Eleanor Roosevelt was a patron.

White legislators, especially those from the southern states where most of the mob executions took place, resisted efforts to pass federal laws against lynching. Roosevelt supported the passage of a federal antilynching bill and encouraged her husband to do the same. Although her persistence finally swayed FDR, she was only able to elicit a lukewarm endorsement, since the president knew that his supporters in the South considered the antilynching bill an unconstitutional intrusion into state affairs. As Franklin Roosevelt told Walter White, the head of the NAACP, "If I come out for the anti-lynching bill now, [southerners] will block every bill I ask Congress to pass to keep America from collapsing. I just can't take the risk."

Indeed, as Eleanor Roosevelt was well aware, it was a risky proposition indeed to support civil rights for blacks in the 1930s. Racists labeled her a "nigger-lover" and sent her vicious letters attacking her behavior. As Democratic politician Adlai Stevenson said of Roosevelt in 1963, "Long before the civil rights issue moved to the forefront of the nation's consciousness, she was there, earning public abuse for her quiet reminders of the inequalities practiced in our land." Taking racial bigotry for granted, some of her opponents simply circulated photographs of the first lady with a black child at a slum clearance project or visiting a black college. Although the sight of America's first lady associating with people of different races horrified some people, Roosevelt refused to pay them any attention. When questioned about the pictures, she replied that they had been taken with her permission, and that she did not object to their distribution.

Racism was so ingrained in U.S. society that even Eleanor Roosevelt occasionally needed to be reminded that she was practicing it on an unconscious level. But unlike many other Americans, she examined her attitudes and worked to obliterate the last vestiges of prejudice. For example, she realized that she did not greet her friend Mary McLeod Bethune with a kiss, as she did many of her white friends. Afterwards, she made a conscious decision to treat Bethune as she did her other close acquaintances, and soon found that she was kissing her hello without thinking about it at all.

Roosevelt's choice of language was another personal matter that had larger political implications than she initially grasped. Even as she worked to improve the daily lives of black Americans, she still referred to them with words she had learned in her youth—terms such as *pickaninny* and *darky*. A young black woman once told Roosevelt that she "couldn't believe my eyes" when she came across these words in the first lady's writings. Roosevelt's response to this criticism demonstrated her willingness to rectify her mistake: " 'Darky' was used by my Georgia great aunt as a term of affection and I have always considered it in that light. I am sorry if it hurt you. What do you prefer?"

Without a doubt, Eleanor Roosevelt was one of black America's most stalwart champions during a volatile time for race relations. Whether making

Roosevelt dictates "My Day" to her secretary. This daily newspaper column, which she began in 1935, described the first lady's concerns and activities.

This official portrait shows FDR with his top advisers. Labor Secretary Frances Perkins (back row, far right) was the first woman ever to serve on a presidential cabinet.

sure blacks were included in FDR's New Deal, working for integrated housing, or resigning from the DAR when that organization banned Marian Anderson from its concert hall, Eleanor Roosevelt came through for blacks. Felix Frankfurter, who served on the Supreme Court from 1939 to 1962, complimented Roosevelt on her refusal to give in to "racebaiters and exploiters of unreason" and pointed out that she rendered "deep service to the enduring values of civilization by serving the nation as a historic example of simple humanity and true human brotherhood in the highest places."

Not only were Roosevelt's views ahead of her time, but she also broke new ground in finding forums for her opinions. In 1935 she began writing a daily syndicated newspaper column entitled "My Day." Even under the most trying circumstances, she always managed to produce her column. Describing the work she and her secretary did on "My Day," Roosevelt commented, "We have written the column while sitting on rocks, eating a picnic lunch, in a slowly moving automobile, on trains, in planes and on ships."

Her editors gave her the latitude to write about anything she wished, or whatever she thought might interest her readers. In the beginning she stuck to such "safe" topics as family life, health, and descriptions of activities at the White House, but she eventually could not resist the opportunity to comment on public affairs. In fact, political observer Arthur Krock once

According to a prominent senator's spouse, Roosevelt's tireless social activism "changed forever the role of political wives in the United States."

joked that if one wanted to know the president's plans one had only to read the first lady's column. Seeking to educate and enlighten her audience, she always refrained from preaching. "I learned a long time ago," she wrote, "that too much crusading for any cause is almost as bad as too little."

Feminism was one of the causes most important to Eleanor Roosevelt, and she continued to urge women to increase their participation in politics.

Largely thanks to the first lady's influence, women occupied more important positions in FDR's administration than ever before in U.S. history. For example, Frances Perkins, whom Eleanor had suggested as New York State labor commissioner, became the first woman to join a presidential cabinet when she became FDR's secretary of labor.

Eleanor Roosevelt's enthusiasm about women in politics was shared and encouraged by Louis Howe, who believed that in the near future a woman could be elected president of the United States. He went so far as to tell her, perhaps only half-jokingly: "If you want to be President in 1940, tell me now so I can start getting things ready." There would come other, more serious, efforts to draft her for the presidency. But she was always quick to respond that one politician in the family was enough. Another reason for Roosevelt's refusal may have been that she thought that the country was not yet ready for a woman president. She hoped, however, that in the future Americans would elect another woman to the nation's highest office, choosing her "as an individual, because of her capacity and the trust which a majority of the people have in her integrity and ability as a person."

But as much as she accomplished in the White House, Eleanor Roosevelt never felt truly at home there. She once remarked that when she broke a dish she felt as if she was breaking a piece of history. And just as she had feared, she had to curtail some of her activities because some traditionalists resented the first lady's activism. She also suffered on a personal level, feeling that she had hardly any time for her family, particularly her grown children, who were scattered around the country. Nonetheless, she always managed to go to them if they needed her. When Franklin, Jr., called from Virginia after an auto accident, she was there in two hours; when James underwent stomach surgery, she was by his side in a Minnesota hospital.

Franklin Roosevelt ran for reelection in 1936, and Eleanor accompanied him on his campaign tours. Because of FDR's popularity, it was not a difficult campaign, but it did require a lot of work. At a Philadelphia women's breakfast, Labor Secretary Frances Perkins summed up the first lady's contribution to both FDR's presidency and his campaign: "She has gone out courageously, in the face of unfavorable criticism, not only to meet the people as a friend but to use that contact to make of herself a channel through which the needs and hopes and desires of people could be carried to places where solutions could be found to their problems. If ever there was a gallant and courageous and intelligent and wise woman, she is one."

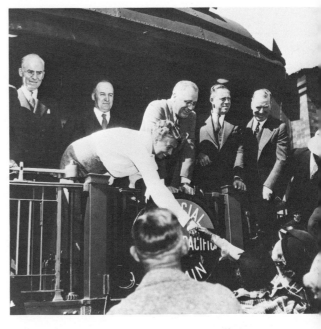

Accompanying her husband on the 1936 campaign trail, Eleanor Roosevelt greets an admirer. She soon began another four-year term as an activist first lady.

FDR was reelected by a landslide, and Eleanor resumed her duties as first lady, activist, and social commentator. In 1937 she published her first book, a best-selling volume of recollections entitled *This Is My Story*. When she saw the first bound copy of her book she happily exclaimed, "It looks much more important than I had ever imagined it would be." She later remarked that the book's success gave her special pleasure because it marked the first time she received recognition on her own and not through her association with her husband.

Italian leader Benito Mussolini (left) and German dictator Adolf Hitler (right) joined with Japan to form the Axis powers, nations whose aggressive expansionism led to World War II.

SEVEN

Life During Wartime

Franklin Delano Roosevelt and his administration used democratic institutions to guide the United States through economic hard times, but leaders such as Germany's Adolf Hitler and Italy's Benito Mussolini used another system to govern their troubled countries: a brand of right-wing dictatorship known as fascism. Both men used tactics of fear, emotional appeals to national pride, and prejudice to build and maintain control over their populations. Hitler and Mussolini also shared a desire for conquest. As FDR's second term drew to a close, the German army had invaded and occupied Poland, Denmark, Norway, Belgium, Holland, and France. The conflict that would become known as World War II had begun.

On the domestic front, Franklin Roosevelt had been nominated for an unprecedented third term. As he campaigned across the country, FDR publicly pledged to keep America out of the war in Europe, although privately he feared that this would prove impossible. Eleanor Roosevelt was worried about the toll that the presidency was taking on both her husband and herself, but she supported his resolution to stay at the helm at a time of world crisis.

The first lady played a pivotal role at the 1940 Democratic National Convention in Chicago. As soon as the conference opened, the delegates found a great deal to disagree about, particularly FDR's choice for his running mate, Henry Wallace. Many Democrats considered Wallace too liberal and thought that he lacked political expertise, but Franklin refused to reconsider his choice. In desperation, Labor Sec-

At the 1940 Democratic National Convention Eleanor Roosevelt gave a moving speech that restored party unity after dissent arose over FDR's choice of running mate.

retary Frances Perkins telephoned Eleanor Roosevelt at Val-Kill and asked her to fly to Chicago and try to restore order at the convention. Roosevelt agreed, and braved the jeering crowd to deliver a sobering speech. "You will have to rise above considerations which are narrow and partisan," she told the assembled delegates. "This is a time when it is the United States we fight for." Wallace's vice-presidential

nomination was confirmed, due largely to the first lady's influence. The next day the headline for an article on the convention proclaimed: MRS. ROOSEVELT STILLS THE TUMULT OF 50,000. Senator George Norris wrote Roosevelt that just when it seemed as though "the convention were going to 'blow up' [and] the battle for righteousness was about to be lost, you came on the scene, and what you said in that short speech caused men of sense and honor to stop and think before they plunged.... That one act makes you heroic."

Thanks in part to his wife's efforts, FDR was elected to an unprecedented third term in 1940. The next five years would be a time of crisis for the world, for the United States, and for Franklin and Eleanor Roosevelt. The challenges of those years would cause the first lady to rethink some of her most cherished beliefs.

World War I had taught Eleanor Roosevelt a great deal about the staggering costs of war. She had seen families shattered, lives lost, and young men driven insane by the pressures of battle. As a result, she had become an outspoken pacifist. During the early 1930s she had continued to speak out for peace, but she began to qualify her pleas by the end of the decade. "I am afraid that I am a very realistic pacifist," she wrote. "We can only disarm with other nations: we cannot disarm alone."

Children play amid the rubble of the bombed-out streets of Warsaw, Poland. World War II began after Germany invaded Poland in 1939.

During the late 1930s it had become increasingly clear that Germany, Italy, and Japan—the countries known as the Axis powers—were not disarming but gearing up for full-scale battle. Eleanor Roosevelt had seen the crisis brewing, and in 1938 she published a 47-page booklet entitled *This Troubled World* in which she put forth proposals for international peace-keeping measures. But as the Axis powers embarked on wars of conquest in Europe and the Far East, it became increasingly clear that economic boycotts and diplomatic negotiations were not enough to prevent worldwide warfare.

Much of Europe had fallen to the fascists by mid-1941, when Hitler ordered an invasion of his country's former ally, the Soviet Union. The Soviets then joined Great Britain in its attempts to stave off Hitler's advance. Although the United States still hoped to remain neutral, America was sending aid to the Allies to bolster their efforts against the Axis powers.

In May 1941 FDR established the Office of Civilian Defense (OCD). This agency sought to prepare the nation for the possibility of war. Fiorello La Guardia, the mayor of New York City, was appointed head of the OCD, and Eleanor Roosevelt took on her first official government post when she became the group's deputy director.

On September 7, 1941, just as the OCD's work was beginning to take shape, Sara Delano Roosevelt died. "What ironical things happen in life & how foolish it all seems," Eleanor wrote to a friend. "I looked at my mother-in-law's face after she was dead and understood so many things I'd never seen before. It is dreadful to have lived so close to someone for 36 years & feel no deep affection or sense of loss."

Two months after Sara Roosevelt's death Eleanor scheduled a large luncheon at the Hyde Park estate. She expected Franklin to attend, but he never left his study. At 1:40 P.M. Eleanor learned the reason for FDR's absence. The Japanese had attacked the U.S. naval fleet docked in Pearl Harbor, Hawaii, killing 2,400 people. The day was December 7, 1941, "a date," Franklin Roosevelt said, "that will live in infamy." The bombing meant that America could no longer stay out of the Second World War.

After the United States entered the conflict, Franklin Roosevelt went on a diplomatic mission to Europe. He suggested that Eleanor undertake a mission of her own, traveling to the South Pacific in an effort to raise the morale of the troops stationed there. She readily agreed to the idea, but objected when she discovered that the proposed itinerary would keep her out of the most dangerous parts of the war zone. She felt that her trip would be in vain if she was prohibited from visiting the places where thousands of servicemen were risking their lives every day. Her goal was to see the island of Guadalcanal, the scene of some of the most desperate fighting in the Pacific.

Admiral William "Bull" Halsey—one of the toughest commanders in the navy—balked at having a woman, especially the wife of the president, prowling about his domain. According to Halsey's own account, as soon as the first lady stepped off the airplane in Noumea, New Caledonia, he gruffly asked her about her plans. When she asked him for suggestions, he proposed that she visit New Zealand and Australia, where the Allied forces felt somewhat neglected because they were not fighting on the front lines. Roosevelt approved of the plan, and hopefully mentioned the possibility of visiting Guadalcanal as well. Halsey made his views clear. "Guadalcanal," he tersely told the first lady, "is no place for you, Ma'am." Dismissing Roosevelt's assurances that she would take complete responsibility for her own well-being, the admiral insisted that he could not spare a plane to take her to Guadalcanal. He would, however, post-

A U.S. destroyer explodes during the Japanese attack on Pearl Harbor, Hawaii. The United States declared war on the Axis powers after the December 7, 1941, bombing.

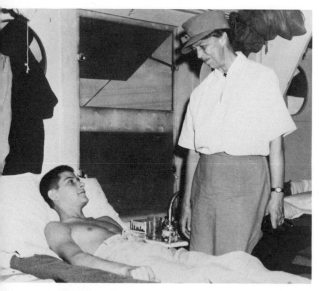

Eleanor Roosevelt comforts a wounded soldier in a Fiji Islands hospital during her morale-boosting 1943 trip to the Pacific battlefront.

pone his final decision until she returned from the rest of her trip.

Despite his original brusqueness, Halsey quickly warmed to the first lady during her stay in New Caledonia. He was astonished by the vigorous way she went about her business. "When I say she inspected those hospitals," he wrote, "I don't mean that she shook hands with the chief medical officer, glanced into a sun parlor, and left. I mean that she went into every ward, stopped at every bed, and spoke to every patient: What was his name? How did he feel? Was there anything he needed? Could she take a message home for him?" If a soldier mentioned that she had spoken at his commence-

ment, or that he had attended a speech she had given, Roosevelt would ask where he was from and try to remember something about his hometown. Roosevelt had four sons and one son-in-law in active service, and she responded to the young men whom she met overseas with genuine maternal warmth. "She reminded one more of some boy's mother back home," one soldier remarked, "than the wife of the President of the United States—and we all loved it."

In New Zealand she continued her rounds of hospitals, Red Cross canteens, camps, official receptions, and munitions factories. She also tried to see something of the country and its people. She made a special effort to stop at Rotorua, the home of the Maoris, a Polynesian people native to the island. Introduced to her guide, Rangi, Roosevelt adopted the traditional Maori greeting, rubbing her nose against her new friend's. When she left, the Maoris dubbed her "Kotoku," or "the White Heron of the One Flight." According to native folklore, this extraordinary creature is seen but once in a lifetime.

When Roosevelt arrived back at Noumea, she was delighted to learn that she had finally been granted permission to visit Guadalcanal. "Gosh, there's Eleanor," the first lady heard a young soldier exclaim after she landed on the island. Noting that the officer escorting her was "plainly horrified to

Roosevelt and a serviceman examine wrecked warplanes on the island of Guadalcanal, the scene of some of the Pacific front's most heated combat.

have me treated with such levity," the first lady assured him that she felt honored by the soldier's enthusiastic, if informal, exclamation.

The island had been bombed by the Japanese the day before Eleanor Roosevelt's arrival, and it would be bombed again the day after she left. An air-raid alert sounded just as she reached the hospital she planned to visit. The first lady and her companions dove for shelter alongside many of the patients. After the all clear sounded, she brushed herself off and calmly made her rounds.

Roosevelt's overseas trip drew criticism at home. Some charged that her journey diverted attention and resources away from the battlefront, or that it was simply a public relations campaign by FDR's administration. But others—particularly the soldiers she visited in bases and hospitals across the Pacific—saw her trip as a selfless act of mercy. As Eleanor Roosevelt left for home, Admiral Halsey confessed that he was "ashamed of my original surliness. She alone had accomplished more good than any other person, or any group of civilians, who had passed through my area."

Fifty-nine-year-old Eleanor Roosevelt lost 30 pounds on her grueling 23,000-mile Pacific trip. She covered 17

Adopting the traditional native greeting, Roosevelt rubs noses with her Maori guide during a visit to New Zealand, part of her 23,000-mile Pacific trip.

islands and saw some 400,000 men in camps and hospitals. The whole time she had faithfully turned out her syndicated daily column, and when she returned to the United States she gave full reports on her findings to her husband and to Red Cross officials. She was exhausted from her journey but knew that more work had to be done.

Franklin Roosevelt triumphed over his Republican opponent, Thomas E. Dewey, in the 1944 presidential election. His fourth term began as World War II was finally drawing to a close. As the nation felt a resurgence of hope and began to plan for the future, the president who had seen America through the war was ailing. He was spending more and more time at a spa in Warm Springs, Georgia, where he tried to recover his lost vigor. His battle ended on April 12, 1945, when he died of a cerebral hemorrhage just 82 days into his fourth presidential term.

On that fateful day Eleanor Roosevelt was speaking in Washington. She received a telephone call from Steve Early, one of her husband's closest associates. She related in her 1949 memoir *This I Remember* that he "asked me to come home at once. I did not even ask why." She recalled that as she traveled to the White House, "In my heart of hearts I knew what had happened, but one does not actually formulate these terrible thoughts until they are spoken."

After she learned of her husband's death, Eleanor Roosevelt remained calm, thinking more of others than about her personal loss. One of the first things she did was send a cable to her sons: DARLINGS: FATHER SLEPT AWAY THIS AFTERNOON. HE DID HIS JOB TO THE END AS HE WOULD WANT YOU TO DO. Vice-president Harry S. Truman was summoned to the White House and escorted into Eleanor's sitting room. As biographer Joseph Lash reported in *Eleanor and Franklin*, the two of them had a frank exchange. "Harry," Roosevelt said, "the president is dead." When Truman asked her if there was anything he could do for her, she replied with a question of her own. "Is there anything *we* can do for *you?*" she asked evenly. "For you are the one in trouble now."

Eleanor Roosevelt had what she described as an "almost impersonal feeling" about Franklin's death. Her reaction was probably due in part to her discovery that FDR had resumed his affair with Lucy Mercer, who had been with him when he died. Her disappointment in her marriage—and her ability to come to grips with these feelings—is apparent in this passage from *This I Remember*:

> All human beings have failings, all human beings have needs and temptations and stresses. Men and women who live together through long years get to know one another's failings; but they also come to know what is worthy of respect and admiration in those they live with and in themselves. If at the end one can say: "This man used to the limit the powers that God granted him; he was worthy of love and respect and of the sacrifices of many people, made in order that he might achieve what he deemed to be his task," then that life had been lived well and there are no regrets.
>
> He might have been happier with a wife who was completely uncritical. That I was never able to be, and he had to find it in some other people. Nevertheless, I think that I sometimes acted as a spur, even though the spurring was not always wanted nor welcome. I was one of those who served his purposes.

Flanked by his son James Roosevelt and Vice-President Truman (left), FDR delivers his fourth inaugural address in January 1945. He died three months later.

After Eleanor Roosevelt moved out of the White House, she seemed emotionally drained, ready to slip into obscurity. When questioned one afternoon by a reporter, Roosevelt waived her away. "The story is over," she said. In reality, however, though one story had ended, another was just beginning.

A veiled Eleanor Roosevelt is supported by her daughter, Anna, as she attends her husband's burial in Hyde Park, New York.

EIGHT

United Nations Delegate

After FDR's death Eleanor Roosevelt returned to her family's Hyde Park estate. Instead of moving into the big house, in which she had never felt comfortable, she chose to live simply in Val-Kill cottage. There she found solace in long walks with Fala, Franklin's Scotch terrier. Little by little, she recovered her physical strength and emotional vigor. As she mastered her feelings and began to look to the future, Roosevelt encouraged other Americans to do the same. She resumed her "My Day" column shortly after FDR's death, telling her readers that "the Almighty is trying to show us that a leader may chart the way, may point out the road to lasting peace, but that many leaders and many peoples must do the building."

Four months after FDR's passing World War II ended in an Allied victory.

Eleanor Roosevelt immediately began to work on achieving the "lasting peace" for which she and millions of other war-weary people longed. Ever since World War I, she had argued that the United States should be part of an international peacekeeping body, and she saw her dream fulfilled in 1945 when the United Nations was created. That same year President Truman asked her to serve as a delegate to the UN's General Assembly, the branch of the organization in which representatives from the world's countries would debate international affairs. The group would convene in London, and Eleanor Roosevelt agreed to attend its first meeting. She was the only woman in the U.S. delegation.

Filled with high hopes—and trepidation because of her lack of foreign-policy experience—Roosevelt sailed

Eleanor Roosevelt takes a stroll with Fala. During FDR's lifetime, Secret Service agents nicknamed the Scottie "the Informer" because his presence heralded the president's arrival.

across the Atlantic late in 1945. She used the trip to prepare herself for the diplomatic challenges ahead. She read through government documents late into each night and attended an array of meetings and state department briefings. "I was feeling rather lost," she later wrote of this time, "and quite uncertain about what lay ahead."

Roosevelt's fears were hardly allayed by colleagues such as future secretary of state John Foster Dulles and U.S.

senator Arthur Vandenberg, neither of whom had much confidence in her abilities. At her first delegation meeting she learned that she had been assigned to work on Committee 3, which would deal with humanitarian problems. In her book *On My Own*, Roosevelt imagined how her skeptical associates decided to assign her to Committee 3: "We can't put Mrs. Roosevelt on the political committee. What could she do on the budget committee? Does she know anything about legal questions? Ah, here's the safe spot for her—Committee 3. She can't do much harm there!"

But contrary to some expectations, Committee 3—and Eleanor Roosevelt—turned out to be a very important part of the United Nations. In 1946 she was appointed head of the Commission on Human Rights, a subdivision of Committee 3 that was meeting in New York. The commission was created to draft a Universal Declaration of Human Rights. This task seemed straightforward at first, but as Roosevelt was soon to discover, the delegates would argue over every point—and nearly every word.

Article 1, for example, opened with the statement that "All men are created equal." Women from the Indian delegation pointed out that this language seemed to leave women out completely and voiced fears that it would reinforce the discrimination they encountered at home. After they met with Roosevelt the phrase was changed to "All human beings." Meanwhile, the Soviet delegation, led by the imposing Andrei Vishinsky, objected to a different word in the article, the verb *created*. Vishinsky maintained that this word implied the existence of a divine being, a concept rejected by his nation's communist government. *Created* was finally changed to *born*. The delegation debated these and other points for hours every day, and as the com-

mittee's leader, Roosevelt demanded much of her colleagues. After an especially grueling meeting, the representative from Panama half-jokingly asked her not to forget the human rights of the members of the commission.

Although she had been criticized as a "merciless slave driver" by some of her associates, Roosevelt still managed to enjoy some lighthearted moments. Joseph Lash reported that one day, while walking through the marble halls of the commission's headquarters, Roosevelt had remarked to fellow delegate James Hendrick that she would "love to slide on these floors." Months later, after the commission finally adopted the declaration by a 13 to 4

United Nations delegate Roosevelt meets with colleagues (left to right) Senator Arthur Vandenberg, Edward Stettinius, and Senator Tom Connally as their ship docks in England in 1946.

vote, the two of them were leaving the building when Hendrick turned to her and said, "Now you can take your slide." Eleanor Roosevelt took a running start and slid down the marble corridor. She liked it so much she did it again.

Roosevelt's two years of hard work on the Universal Declaration of Human Rights came to an end on December 10, 1948, when the General Assembly voted to approve the document after hours of debate. Once their work was done the exhausted but jubilant delegates rose and gave Roosevelt an unprecedented standing ovation. Even her old foe, Senator Arthur Vandenberg, commented, "I want to say that I take back everything I ever said about her." He added wryly, "And believe me, it's been plenty."

Aside from the Universal Declaration of Human Rights, Roosevelt's primary concern during this period was helping those Europeans still suffering from the devastating effects of World War II. Both as a private citizen and as a UN delegate, she supported efforts to restore prosperity to the war-torn continent. She also worked on behalf of the more than one million refugees inhabiting overcrowded camps in Germany, Austria, France, and Italy. These individuals had survived the Nazi concentration camps or had been forced to leave their homes as the war spread.

Because Adolf Hitler's government had systematically tried to eliminate the Jews of Europe, many of these refugees were Jewish. Roosevelt had visited some of their camps, where she witnessed firsthand the pain and despair of the inhabitants. "Every face I saw seemed to represent a story more tragic than the last," she wrote. In her memoirs, Roosevelt described a moving encounter that took place in the city of Zilcheim, Germany: "In the mud of Zilcheim I remember an old woman whose family had been driven from home by war and madness and brutality. I had no idea who she was and we could not speak each other's language. But she knelt in the muddy road and threw her arms around my knees. 'Israel,' she murmured over and over, 'Israel! Israel!'" Roosevelt said that after this incident, she knew "for the first time what that small land meant to so many, many people."

Although Roosevelt felt great sympathy for the Jews, she had been slow to accept the Zionist position that they needed a homeland of their own. "Why," she once asked, "can't Jews be members of the religious body but natives of the land in which they live?" When it became clear that most countries, including the United States, were not willing to take in large numbers of Jewish refugees, she began to look more carefully at the idea of establishing a Jewish homeland in Palestine, a region in the Middle East.

In February 1947 Great Britain, the country governing Palestine, turned the question of the region's future over to the United Nations. After many delays the UN Special Committee on Palestine issued a report calling for the end of British rule in the region. Palestine would be separated into two independent states: one Jewish, one Arab. The UN's Arab delegates protested the proposal, insisting that the entire area was rightfully theirs. Eleanor Roosevelt, however, was pleased with the plan. "Justice," she insisted, "cannot be for one side alone, but must be for both." The General Assembly approved the partition on November 29, 1947, by a 33 to 13 vote, with 10 countries abstaining.

Roosevelt felt strongly that the UN's

Eleanor Roosevelt listens to a translation of a UN associate's remarks. Despite her lack of foreign-policy experience, she quickly proved herself an able diplomat.

Roosevelt displays the Universal Declaration of Human Rights, approved by the UN in 1948. She headed the committee that drafted this historic international agreement.

decision should be supported by the United States. She wrote that "it would be a blow to the prestige of the United Nations from which it would never recover, if they do not implement their decision, and if we do not do our share we will be responsible for sabotaging the only machinery we have for having peace today." But the U.S. government was wavering on the partition plan, and President Truman was unwilling to send American peace-keeping troops into Palestine. Exasperated, Roosevelt offered to resign her position as "a small cog in our work at the UN." Soon afterwards, Truman did an about-face and publicly proclaimed that "Israel must be large enough and strong enough to make its people self-supporting and secure."

In May 1948 the British formally withdrew from Palestine, and the state of Israel was proclaimed. Roosevelt later reported that when the Israeli flag was raised alongside those of the other UN countries, "There was a lump in almost everybody's throat, I think, at the thought of a new nation being born and one whose people had suffered greatly." Roosevelt visited Israel several times, and she worked to raise money for the struggling country, which was attacked by surrounding Arab states as soon as it came into existence. She wrote articles and gave speeches in support of the people of Israel and donated the proceeds from a lecture tour to the United Jewish Appeal.

The same year that Israel was created Clare Boothe Luce, a former Republican congresswoman, offered the Democrats some advice for the upcoming election. The only chance they had of winning, she said, was with a Harry S. Truman-Eleanor Roosevelt ticket. Roosevelt laughed off the suggestion. But although she did not run as his vice-president, Truman carried the election in 1948—in part, perhaps, because she had supported him in the race. By this time, she was one of the most celebrated and respected women in the world. Her name had been appearing regularly in each year's Gallup poll on the women most admired in the United States, and a 1948 popularity survey in the *Woman's Home Companion* placed her at the top of a

Through diplomacy and private charity, Roosevelt worked to aid the victims of World War II, such as these survivors of the Nazi concentration camp Buchenwald.

Hopeful Jews arrive in Palestine in 1947. Before the founding of Israel, most such refugees were turned away from the land where they hoped to build new lives.

Roosevelt tours an Israeli settlement in 1959. Israel was created in 1948 after the UN devised a plan to divide Palestine into two nations, one Jewish, one Arab.

Roosevelt and President Truman discuss state affairs after a memorial service for FDR. She entered public life because of her husband but stayed because of her idealism.

list that included political dignitaries and World War II heroes.

Although she was greatly admired, Roosevelt also had her share of detractors. Perhaps her most vicious opponent was ultraconservative columnist Westbrook Pegler, who began his attacks during her term as first lady and continued them after she left the White House. Pegler used a wide arsenal of unflattering names to refer to Roosevelt. He called her *La Boca Grande* (the Big Mouth), the Gab, and Roosevelt the Great. He also referred to her as "the daughter of a drunkard" and implied that she was a communist. Roosevelt seldom responded to Pegler's onslaughts. When asked about her attitude, she explained, "I have learned that the only way to cope with unfair critics is to ignore them and not to lower oneself by answering back."

She found another adversary, Roman Catholic leader Francis Cardinal Spellman, more difficult to ignore. Spellman was an outspoken advocate of federal aid to church-run schools, which Roosevelt opposed on the grounds that such aid would breach the Constitution's doctrine of the separation of church and state. In a 1949 newspaper column, she tactfully took issue with Cardinal Spellman on the parochial school issue. The cardinal, who had long disapproved of her outspoken views, particularly her support of birth control, exploded in an open letter to Roosevelt. He wrote that he considered her piece a personal attack and accused her of conducting an "anti-Catholic campaign." He concluded his letter: "And even though you may use your columns to attack me and accuse me of starting a controversy, I shall not again publicly acknowledge you. For, whatever you may say in the future, your record of anti-Catholicism stands for all to see—a record which you yourself wrote in the pages of history which cannot be recalled—documents of discrimination unworthy of an American mother."

The cardinal's letter elicited public outcry, and the mail to Hyde Park ran nine to one in Roosevelt's favor. Even at the risk of alienating some Catholic voters, many prominent officials supported her right to state her views. Roosevelt's friend, poet Archibald MacLeish, wrote a stinging verse about the cardinal's attack. Quoting Spellman, he entitled it "I Shall Not Again Publicly Acknowledge You."

In her "My Day" column, Roosevelt told her readers that Cardinal Spellman had written "in what to him seems a Christian and kindly manner and I wish to do the same." She opted to answer him in a personal letter that gently chided him for judging others so harshly. "I assure you," she wrote, "that I had no sense of being an 'unworthy American mother.' The final judgment, my dear Cardinal Spellman, of the unworthiness of all human beings is in the hands of God."

Finally Spellman sent word that he wished to speak with her. When asked if she would be willing to meet with him, she reminded her questioner, "I'm not the one who said I would have nothing to do with the cardinal." Spellman visited her at Hyde Park one evening, and the two of them had a friendly and polite exchange. The next day the rift ended when Cardinal Spellman issued a statement noting "the great confusion and regrettable misunderstandings" that had arisen. He also acknowledged "the American right of free speech which not only permits but encourages differences of opin-

Cardinal Francis Spellman labeled Roosevelt an unfit mother when she opposed federal aid to church-run schools. The two leaders finally agreed to disagree.

ion." But the resolution of her battle with the cardinal did not mark the end of her career as a controversial public figure. At 65 years of age, Eleanor Roosevelt had no plans to abandon her lifelong practice of standing up for her beliefs.

Eleanor Roosevelt enjoys a rare moment of repose in her New York City home. She continued to work for international cooperation and individual rights well into her seventies.

NINE

"Life Was Meant to Be Lived"

When she was traveling in the Pacific during World War II, Eleanor Roosevelt's code name, bestowed affectionately by FDR, had been Rover. Years later she still had not slowed her pace. During her stint as an American delegate to the UN, she traveled to many of the emerging countries known as the Third World. She made a real effort to understand the traditions and needs of other nations, in contrast to some American politicians. "We're not living in an American world," she reminded her fellow diplomats. Although many people in the places she visited were skeptical of a representative from a superpower such as the United States, her genuine concern managed to win over many of those she met. But warmth was not all that

she had to offer: Roosevelt was also a hard-headed analyst of international affairs. When an interviewer for the Voice of America network asked an Indonesian diplomat who could best comment on a pending treaty, the answer came quickly: Eleanor Roosevelt.

President Truman often took advantage of Roosevelt's diplomatic abilities, and early in 1952 he asked her to accept Indian prime minister Jawaharlal Nehru's standing invitation to visit his country. En route, she stopped off in Beirut, Lebanon, and was saddened to find that the Arabs she spoke with there still talked of dissolving the nation of Israel.

As her plane approached Karachi, Pakistan, a traveling companion ex-

Roosevelt meets with Indian prime minister Jawaharlal Nehru (left) and diplomat Shrimati Vijayalakshmi during her 1952 visit to India, undertaken at President Truman's request.

claimed "Look!" and Roosevelt glanced out the window to see a huge crowd of people gathered at the airport. "That's not for us," she said in disbelief. But when she learned that the "sea of women" was indeed there to honor her, Roosevelt modestly remarked that she "hadn't realized how they cared about Franklin." After visiting Pakistan she moved on to India, where she addressed the national parliament before going to Indonesia. Secretary of State Dean Acheson later sent the president a glowing memo on her mission: "Although it was undertaken in a purely unofficial capacity, Mrs. Roose-velt's journey has served the public interest exceedingly well."

Roosevelt also continued to work for international accord as a United Nations delegate during this period. Because the 1948 Universal Declaration of Human Rights was simply a statement of principles, she and her colleagues on the Human Rights Commission embarked on the difficult task of drafting an international accord with legal binding power. It would be difficult to strike such a ground-breaking agreement under any circumstances, but, as Roosevelt would find out, it was impossible to do so in the climate of distrust that arose between the United States and the Soviet Union after World War II. The cold war, as this period of heightened U.S.-Soviet tension was called, would ultimately stall the Human Rights Commission's attempts.

During the negotiations on the Covenant on Human Rights, the delegates from the Soviet Union used the proceedings to attack the United States. They charged that the American government was indifferent to social and economic rights both at home and around the world. Roosevelt calmly listened to their charges, which they supported with distorted figures she later termed "statistical caricatures." She answered the accusations one by one and then turned the tables on the Soviet delegates by subtly pointing to the restrictions imposed by the government of the U.S.S.R. "I wish it were possible for all of us to be allowed to go to the Soviet Union, for example, to see for ourselves the actual conditions which exist there."

Roosevelt found that progress on the Covenant on Human Rights was blocked in the United States as well. Although she gave lectures, wrote articles, and used her daily column to explain the work of the United Nations, many Americans remained skeptical about the peace-keeping body. Some thought that the UN was a futile waste of tax dollars; others objected to the idea of becoming involved in international agreements—especially with the

Roosevelt conducts a television discussion on the atomic bomb. The panel included scientist J. Robert Oppenheimer (far right), one of the weapon's developers.

Soviets. When the U.S. Senate refused to ratify the covenant, Roosevelt was disheartened. "I do not understand what is happening to us," she said, "whether it is a purely isolationist movement or whether it is fear . . . and I am tired of being afraid."

Roosevelt was still fighting for the covenant in the summer of 1952, when she gave a moving speech at the Democratic National Convention. As soon as the delegates spotted her coming down the aisle, they rose and roared their approval, and the band struck up "Happy Days Are Here Again," the Democratic party theme song associated with FDR and the New Deal. Seeing her difficulty in speaking over the din of the crowd, the chairman banged on his desk: "Will the delegates please take their seats. Several million people are waiting to hear the First Lady of the World." Speaking of the Covenant on Human Rights and United Nations in general, she insisted that without the UN's efforts, "our country would walk alone, ruled by fear instead of confidence and hope. To weaken or hamstring the United Nations now, through lack of faith and lack of vision, would be to condemn ourselves to endless struggle for survival in a jungle world." The day after the convention, the New York *Post's* front page blared: MRS. FDR STOPS THE SHOW.

The Democrats had chosen Adlai Stevenson as their party's presidential

Political advisers Bernard Baruch and John Foster Dulles look on as Roosevelt receives an award for her "contribution to the cause of harmony."

nominee. Roosevelt wholeheartedly supported Stevenson, a former UN colleague whom she characterized as someone who "knows more about the world than almost any other man in this country." She was disappointed that November when Republican Dwight D. Eisenhower was the victor in the presidential contest.

Roosevelt offered to resign from the UN so that Eisenhower could "feel free to appoint a Republican woman." Few expected that the new president would accept her offer, but surprisingly, he did. According to some accounts, the former war hero believed that Roosevelt had made some unkind personal remarks about his wife—remarks that all agree are unlikely ever to have been uttered by a woman as kind and tactful as Roosevelt—and for that reason was reluctant to work with her. To her dismay, once she was gone the U.S. delegation to the UN ceased its efforts on behalf of the Covenant on Human Rights.

But Eleanor Roosevelt would not give up on the UN, or on the organization's goals to provide relief to the poor, promote international understanding, and work for peace. In early 1953 she appeared unexpectedly at the office of Dr. Clark Eichelberger, director of the American Association for the United Nations (AAUN), a group supporting the UN's efforts. As Joseph Lash described the meeting in *Eleanor: The Years Alone*, Roosevelt approached

Senator Joseph McCarthy testifies at a 1954 Washington hearing. Although his anticommunist crusades cowed many Americans, Roosevelt spoke out against his witch-hunt.

Eichelberger in her usual straightforward manner. "Do you think," she asked him, "You could use me in your association as an educational volunteer?" Eichelberger was dumbfounded and reported that he "practically fell on the floor." Needless to say, he accepted her offer.

When Roosevelt joined the AAUN she told Eichelberger that she had plans to take another trip around the world, in June and July. She spent six weeks in Japan, where she became concerned about the status of women in that country. After that she went to Hong Kong, India, Pakistan, Turkey, and Greece. President Tito of Yugosla-

via and his wife entertained her on their private Adriatic island, where Roosevelt and the socialist leader had searching discussions on international relations.

But opening channels for international understanding and cooperation was not Roosevelt's only interest during this period: She was concerned and distressed by developments at home. The distrust many Americans felt toward the Soviet Union began to color domestic politics in the late 1940s and early 1950s. Some politicians, notably Wisconsin senator Joseph McCarthy, began to charge that the United States was harboring a large population of communists bent on undermining the U.S. government. Focusing particularly on public officials and entertainment figures, McCarthy and his supporters unjustly pointed accusing fingers at thousands of Americans. Many of these individuals were then blacklisted—excluded from employment because of their suspected involvement with the Communist party. A frequent target of the red-baiters herself, Roosevelt became the honorary chair of a progressive group called Americans for Democratic Action in order to speak out against McCarthyism.

In 1957 *New York Post* publisher Dorothy Schiff invited Eleanor Roosevelt to travel to the Soviet Union as a correspondent for the newspaper. Always ready to meet a challenge, Roosevelt eagerly accepted. She attended a variety of cultural events, visited museums, and toured farms and cities. Although she learned a great deal during her stay, she was annoyed by the restrictions placed on her itinerary and by the Soviet government's refusal to provide her with accurate statistics on social welfare and the economy.

The highlight of her visit was a two-and-a-half-hour interview with Soviet leader Nikita Khrushchev. Over a meal of Eastern European delicacies, Roosevelt and Khrushchev discussed the cold war, the arms race, and prospects for U.S.-Soviet coexistence. She did not hesitate to challenge Khrushchev, par-

Roosevelt talks with Soviet leader Nikita Khrushchev during her 1957 trip to his country. She felt that communication between the superpowers was essential.

ticularly on the touchy issue of his government's treatment of the nation's Jewish population. As their meeting concluded, he asked, "Can I tell our papers that we have had a friendly conversation?" "Yes," Roosevelt replied, "you can say that we had a friendly conversation but that we differ." The burly Russian was amused. "At least," he joked, "we didn't shoot each other."

After this meeting, Roosevelt invited Khrushchev to visit her Hyde Park home whenever he was in the United States. She was occasionally criticized for socializing with the communist leader, but she insisted on the importance of maintaining both formal and informal lines of communication with the Soviet Union. "We have to face the fact," she insisted, "that either all of us are going to die together or we are going to learn to live together, and if we are to live together we have to talk."

As the 1960 presidential elections approached, Eleanor Roosevelt once again supported Adlai Stevenson, who had unsuccessfully opposed Eisenhower in the past two elections. Hoping that he could once again win the Democratic nomination, she coached him, organized his supporters, and gave speeches and wrote articles touting his abilities. "I have never worked as hard as I have this autumn in our national campaign, but I have enjoyed it very much," the 76-year-old Roosevelt wrote. Her efforts proved fruitless

Eleanor Roosevelt greets former UN colleague Adlai Stevenson. She backed Stevenson's unsuccessful campaigns for the presidency in 1952 and 1956.

when John F. Kennedy became the party's candidate for the presidency.

Kennedy avidly courted Roosevelt's support after winning the nomination. Initially reluctant, she finally agreed to meet with him. Afterwards she wrote, "My final judgement now is that here is a man who wants to leave a record (perhaps for ambitious personal reasons as people say) but I rather think because he is interested in helping the people of his own country and mankind in general." She began to work for his campaign and acted as an informal adviser.

Kennedy won the presidency, and Roosevelt offered him welcome counsel on everything from international

101

relations to his style of speaking. When the 1961 Bay of Pigs invasion of Cuba by the United States failed to overthrow Cuba's communist premier, Fidel Castro, Kennedy appointed Roosevelt to the Tractors for Freedom project. This program was arranged to exchange tractors for American soldiers captured during the ill-fated offensive.

Eleanor Roosevelt's involvement in the Kennedy administration extended even to the president's family. She congratulated his brother, Attorney General Robert F. Kennedy, on his efforts to guarantee the rights and freedoms of black Americans. "You are

By this time a beloved symbol of the Democratic party, a smiling Eleanor Roosevelt acknowledges the cheers of delegates to the 1960 Democratic National Convention.

doing well and the results are gratifying," she wrote him. She also corresponded with the new first lady, Jacqueline Bouvier Kennedy. "I think back to the days of my husband's Presidency," she wrote, "and realize that the problems of that time—first of the depression and then of the war—required a background and understanding of social justice and social needs. That is still needed by the woman in the White House, but much more is required."

During the first year of his presidency, Kennedy reappointed Roosevelt as a delegate to the United Nations. When she entered the UN's General Assembly to resume her duties, the delegates stood and applauded. She later remarked that this unprecedented display of respect and affection was one of the proudest moments of her life.

On her 77th birthday Roosevelt told reporters: "I know I should slow down, but I think I have a good deal of my uncle Theodore in me, because I could not, at any age, be content to take my place in a corner by the fireside and simply look on. Life was meant to be lived. Curiosity must be kept alive. The fatal thing is the rejection. One must never, for whatever reason, turn his back on life."

Eleanor Roosevelt practiced what she preached. Although her health began to fail during her eighth decade, she remained tremendously active.

Democratic nominee John F. Kennedy campaigns in November 1960. After his election, Kennedy reappointed Roosevelt to the UN post she had resigned in 1952.

Aside from her filling her post at the UN, she served as a visiting professor at Brandeis University in Waltham, Massachusetts, where she gave monthly seminars on international affairs. She had a regular television show called "Prospects of Mankind" and even did a television commercial for margarine, donating the proceeds to charity. Roosevelt was also appointed to the National Advisory Council of the Peace Corps, a U.S. government agency that sends volunteers to developing nations. She was asked to chair the Com-

mission on the Status of Women, and she lobbied for the Equal Rights Amendment, a proposed constitutional amendment that would guarantee women "equality of rights under the law." When asked where she found the energy for her myriad pursuits, she replied, "I don't have any more energy than anyone else. But I never waste any of it on regrets."

Roosevelt made her last public appearance at a July 1962 Democratic rally. According to New York politician Ellis Bert's account:

Roosevelt and New York politician Herbert Lehman (left) present an award to civil rights leader Martin Luther King, Jr., in 1961.

A large crowd had gathered in anticipation of Mrs. Roosevelt's appearance. Nearest to the platform were some teenagers wearing buttons of the newly formed Conservative Party. Mrs. Roosevelt arrived about 8:30 P.M. and was greeted with a tumultuous ovation. She was wearing a light blue, print summer dress but her face was pale and she appeared to be quite ill. As she stepped onto the platform to begin her speech, the teenagers started to chant, "Communist, go back to Russia!" Eleanor Roosevelt ignored them. She very forcefully urged the people to vote for the reform ticket and spoke for about fifteen minutes. When she had finished, the boys started their chant again. Mrs. Roosevelt stepped down, went through the crowd to shake hands. Then she murmured "I don't feel very well."

Roosevelt was hospitalized soon after the rally. Tests revealed that she was suffering from a rare form of tuberculosis. Realizing that the end was near, she was determined to spend her last days at home, surrounded by her children. On November 7, 1962, she died at her New York City residence.

Like her husband before her, Anna Eleanor Roosevelt was mourned around the world. "She *lived* equality, freedom, and democracy," Frances Perkins said. "She put those ideals into flesh." Speaking before the United Nations, Adlai Stevenson announced, "I have lost more than a friend, I have lost an inspiration. She would rather light a candle than curse the darkness, and her glow has warmed the world." Apt as Stevenson's words were, the modest Roosevelt probably would best like to be remembered by her favorite tribute, which came from a Maine lobsterman in 1933: "She ain't stuck up, she ain't dressed up, and she ain't afeared to talk."

Roosevelt's last book, published after her death, was entitled *Tomorrow is Now*. In it she challenged America's youth to provide compassionate, farsighted leadership in an increasingly complex world. The achievements of Eleanor Roosevelt—first lady, diplomat, and humanitarian—may well provide a model for future generations who strive to attain that goal.

After a lifetime of fighting injustice and promoting international understanding, Eleanor Roosevelt died of tuberculosis on November 7, 1962.

FURTHER READING

Blassingame, Wyatt. *Eleanor Roosevelt.* New York: Putnam, 1967.

Boller, Paul. *Presidential Wives.* New York: Oxford University Press, 1988.

Hareven, Tamara K. *Eleanor Roosevelt: An American Conscience.* Chicago: Quadrangle Books, 1968.

Hershan, Stella K. *A Woman of Quality: Eleanor Roosevelt.* New York, Crown, 1970.

Hickok, Lorena A. *Eleanor Roosevelt: Reluctant First Lady.* New York: Dodd, Mead, 1962.

———. *The Story of Eleanor Roosevelt.* New York: Grosset & Dunlap, 1959.

Hoff-Wilson, Joan, and Marjorie Lightman, eds. *Without Precedent: The Life and Career of Eleanor Roosevelt.* Bloomington: Indiana University Press, 1984.

Lash, Joseph P. *Eleanor and Franklin.* New York: Norton, 1971.

———. *Eleanor: The Years Alone.* New York: Norton, 1972.

———. *"Life Was Meant to Be Lived": A Centenary Portrait of Eleanor Roosevelt.* New York: Norton, 1984.

———. *Love, Eleanor: Eleanor Roosevelt and Her Friends.* New York: Doubleday, 1982.

McAuley, Karen. *Eleanor Roosevelt.* New York: Chelsea House, 1987.

Roosevelt, Eleanor. *The Autobiography of Eleanor Roosevelt.* New York: Harper & Brothers, 1961.

———. *This I Remember.* New York: Harper & Brothers, 1949.

———. *Tomorrow Is Now.* New York: Harper & Row, 1963.

CHRONOLOGY

Oct. 11, 1884	Anna Eleanor Roosevelt born in New York City
1892	Anna Hall Roosevelt, mother, dies
1894	Elliot Roosevelt, father, dies
1899–1902	Eleanor attends Allenswood, a private girls' school outside London
1905	Marries Franklin Delano Roosevelt, a distant cousin
1906	Gives birth to Anna, the first of six children, five of whom survive infancy
1910	Franklin Roosevelt is elected New York State senator; the family moves to Albany
1917	The United States enters World War I; Eleanor Roosevelt begins volunteer work, cofounding the Navy Relief Society and working for the Red Cross
1920	Joins the League of Women Voters, initiating lifelong involvement in Democratic party politics and women's organizations
1921	Franklin Roosevelt stricken with the polio that cripples him for life
1925	Eleanor Roosevelt cofounds Val-Kill Industries
1927	Teaches at the Todhunter School for Girls
1928	Franklin Roosevelt is elected governor of New York; Eleanor Roosevelt begins inspecting government sites for him
1932	Franklin Roosevelt is elected president; Eleanor Roosevelt begins holding press conferences open only to female correspondents
1935	Eleanor Roosevelt travels to Birmingham, Alabama, to attend a meeting on social and political reform
1936	Starts publishing her newspaper column, "My Day"
1939	World War II begins
1941–42	Roosevelt serves as assistant director of civilian defense
1943	Travels to the South Pacific to boost troop morale
1945	Franklin Roosevelt dies; World War II ends
1945–52	Eleanor Roosevelt serves as a U.S. delegate to the UN; secures passage of Universal Declaration of Human Rights
1952	Undertakes an unofficial diplomatic mission for State Department; travels to India, Pakistan, and the Middle East
1953	President Eisenhower declines to reappoint Roosevelt to the UN
1957	Roosevelt travels to the Soviet Union for the *New York Post*; meets Nikita Khrushchev
1961	President Kennedy reappoints Roosevelt to the UN
Nov. 7, 1962	Eleanor Roosevelt dies of tuberculosis

INDEX

INDEX

INDEX

PICTURE CREDITS

Rachel Toor received a degree in English from Yale University and is currently an editor at a major publishing house in New York City. She is the author of *The Polish Americans,* a volume in Chelsea House's series THE PEOPLES OF NORTH AMERICA.

Matina S. Horner is president of Radcliffe College and associate professor of psychology and social relations at Harvard University. She is best known for her studies of women's motivation, achievement, and personality development. Dr. Horner serves on several national boards and advisory councils, including those of the National Science Foundation, Time Inc., and the Women's Research and Education Institute. She earned her B. A. from Bryn Mawr College and Ph.D. from the University of Michigan, and holds honorary degrees from many colleges and universities, including Mount Holyoke, Smith, Tufts, and the University of Pennsylvania.